COLOR OF RIPE FRUIT

WILD
BERRIES & FRUITS
FIELD GUIDE INDIANA, KENTUCKY AND OHIO

by Teresa Marrone

Adventure Publications, Inc.
Cambridge, MN

ACKNOWLEDGMENTS

Special thanks to Lisa Schindler, for her help with muscadines; to Brian Gasdorf at Natural Bridge State Park in Kentucky; and to Bruce Bohnenstingl, the world's best photo assistant and berry scout.

Thanks to Mike Krebill for his review of the book.

Cover and book design by Jonathan Norberg

Flower anatomy illustration by Julie Martinez

Edited by Brett Ortler

Photo credits by photographer and page number:
Cover photos: Black raspberry by Cindy Seigle; blueberry, buttonbush and rose hips by Teresa Marrone

All photos by Teresa Marrone unless noted.
Steven J. Baskauf: 117 (both), 309 **Will Cook:** 191 (bottom right), 257 **Derek E. Goertz:** 223 (bottom half page) **kenjonbro:** 169 (top half main) **Mike Krebill:** 81 (fruit inset), 207 (inset), 261 **Kris H. Light:** 67, 247 (inset) **Ernie Marx:** 35 **midatlantichikes.com:** 89 (inset) **Robert H. Mohlenbrock/USDA-NRCS PLANTS Database:** 255 (bottom left) **Lorena Babcock Moore:** 217 **Julia Morgan:** 153 (bottom left) **Walter Muma:** 275, 317 (both) **J. S. Peterson:** 203 (fruit inset) **Jesse Ross:** 89 (bottom half page) **Lisa Kelley Schindler:** 45 (main), 193 (both) **Forest and Kim Starr:** 251 (fruit inset) **Ryann Waite:** 65 (inset) **www.chateau-z.com:** 255 (fruit inset) **www.sunfarm.com:** 87

10 9 8 7 6 5 4 3

Wild Berries & Fruits Field Guide of Indiana, Kentucky and Ohio
Copyright © 2011 by Teresa Marrone
Published by Adventure Publications
An imprint of AdventureKEEN
310 Garfield Street South
Cambridge, Minnesota 55008
(800) 678-7006
www.adventurepublications.net
Printed in China
ISBN 978-1-59193-306-9 (pbk.)

TABLE OF CONTENTS

ABOUT THIS BOOK

Numerous field guides are available to aid in flower identification, but few address the fruiting stage of the plant. Those that do usually add a footnote or a small photo of the fruit. But the fruiting stage is critical to the plant and interesting to observers of nature as well. This book is specifically about that glorious stage in a plant's life when it fulfills its purpose by producing fruits to help it reproduce.

This book is unique as it was written with the forager in mind, and especially for foragers interested in taking home their finds and using them in recipes and in the kitchen. For this reason, this book makes references to *Cooking with Wild Berries & Fruits of Indiana, Kentucky and Ohio,* a companion cookbook which includes recipes, handy tips, and different uses for many of the edible species found in this book.

In addition to showing edible berries and fruits, this book also identifies those berries and fruits which are inedible—even toxic. This information is critical to anyone who is faced with an unknown plant and wishes to know if its fruit is edible. It's also just plain interesting to see all the fascinating and, often, lovely fruits produced by plants, whether that fruit is edible or not.

Photos in this book focus primarily on the fruits, in all their up-close-and-personal glory. However, plant structure and leaf form are also critical to proper identification. The photos here attempt to show the key identification points of each plant; this information is also covered in the text that accompanies each photo. Features that are key to distinguishing a plant from one with similar appearance are in green type in the text; study these points with particular care when looking at a plant.

Habitat and season are also important when attempting to identify a plant. Both of these are covered in the text. Range maps for each species show approximate locations in Indiana, Kentucky and Ohio where each plant is likely to be found. Helpful information that allows the reader to compare similar plants provides additional insight that will aid in positive identification. Finally, each plant account includes short notes, which may feature interesting tidbits about the plant, how it has been used for food or medicine, or information on how the plant is used by birds and other wildlife.

Common names of plants are often confusing. People in different areas use different names for the same plant, and, sometimes, the same common name is used for two—or more—very different plants. All plant accounts in this book include the common name usually used by the United States Department of Agriculture, and occasionally another common name. More importantly, the scientific name is listed for each species; this is the most definitive nomenclature of all.

THE RANGE MAPS

The maps showing plant ranges are based on information from the United States Department of Agriculture, the United States Geological Survey, and the United States Forest Service, updated with data from several websites that track invasive plants (see pg. 318 for website addresses). These sources have been supplemented with state-specific surveys from natural-resources agencies, universities and herbariums, as well as the author's personal knowledge and experience.

Range maps are a useful tool, but are not an absolute authority. Plants rarely follow state or county lines, but most plant surveyors do when reporting their data to the USDA or other authorities. Further, some counties have not submitted data or been surveyed, and so do not appear on the lists used by government agencies. The maps in this book are approximations, and it is possible to find a plant in an area not shown on the range map (or, conversely, to be unable to find a plant in an area indicated on the map). In some cases, county-specific data is not available, yet the plant is known to grow in the state. In such cases, the state is colored with a lighter shade of the color used in that section; this indicates that the plant is present in the state, but does not show specific areas where it may be found.

WHAT IS A FRUIT?

Since this book is all about fruit, it's worth discussing exactly what that term means in the context of the book. At its most basic, a fruit is the ripened part of a plant that disperses seeds; this includes things like pea pods, wheat heads and nuts. In everyday usage, however, most of us consider only fleshy, juicy, seed-bearing structures, such as blueberries, watermelon and apples, to be "fruit." The short and fairly non-scientific discussion that follows will provide helpful reference for the discussion of various fruit types discussed later.

Like most living things, plants have male and female parts. Depending on species, they may exist together in one flower as illustrated below, or may grow in distinct male or female flowers. (Sometimes the male and female parts don't look anything like this, as with pine trees; then again, these plants don't produce what we think of as fruit.) The female part of the plant, at the center of the flower, is collectively called the *pistil*. It consists of an ovary, topped with a long style, capped with the stigma. The ovary is a case containing one or more carpels, which are ovule-bearing structures containing one or more ovules, or eggs; typically, several carpels are fused together within the ovary, but in a few cases the carpel is single.

The male part of the plant is collectively called the *stamen*. It consists of the pollen-bearing element called the anther, which is supported by the filament, a thin structure that raises the anther above the base of the flower. (The flower petals are there to attract pollinators, by the way—the plant world's version of the little black dress.)

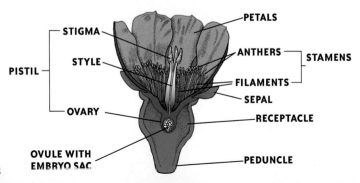

Seeds develop when pollen is introduced into ripe eggs. This service is performed by insects, animals or the wind; regardless of the method, the pollen is deposited onto the sticky stigma, where it germinates, sending the male nuclei down the style to fertilize the eggs. The ovary swells as the seeds mature. The result of all this activity is the fruit—a fleshy structure carrying the fertilized seeds.

Within that narrow definition, there are several types of fruit. Here are short, simple definitions of the types of fruits that are included in this book; please also look at page 19 to see what is *not* included.

BERRIES

A berry is a simple fleshy fruit containing one or more carpels (ovule-bearing structures), each with one or more seeds. The seed coating, or endocarp, is relatively soft. Examples include grapes (pgs. 190, 192, 254), gooseberries (pgs. 48, 198, 266), currants (pgs. 128, 268) and blueberries (pgs. 218, 224).

Grapes

Gooseberries

Currants

Blueberries

DRUPES

A drupe, sometimes called a stone fruit, is a simple fleshy fruit with a seed (or on occasion, seeds) contained in a hard pit, or stone. The hard outside of the pit is the endocarp (seed coating). Examples include plums (pgs. 174, 176, 208), autumn olives (pg. 154) and chokecherries (pg. 148).

American wild plum

Autumn olive

Common chokecherry

COMPOUND DRUPES

A compound drupe is a fleshy fruit formed from a single flower, but composed of many drupes, each containing one seed. Compound drupes are typically thought of as "seedy" because they contain so many seeds, each with its own endocarp (seed coating). Examples include red raspberries (pg. 124) and blackberries (pg. 272).

Red raspberry

Blackberry

Mulberry

MULTIPLE FRUIT

An unusual fruit structure in which a single fruit is formed from multiple flowers that grow closely together in a cluster. Multiple fruits in this book are Osage orange (pg. 54) and mulberries (pg. 166). Figs and pineapples are multiple fruits that don't grow in our region.

POMES

A pome is a pseudocarp, a simple fruit with flesh developed from the receptacle (the end of the flower stalk) rather than the ovary. In pomes, the receptacle surrounds the ovary, and seeds are contained in the carpel, which becomes papery. Examples in this book include crabapples (pg. 170), hawthorns (pg. 180), mountain ash (pg. 78) and serviceberries (pg. 204).

Crabapple

Hawthorn

Mountain ash

Serviceberry

OTHER TYPES OF FRUIT

Strawberry

Pseudocarps are fruits whose flesh develops from a part other than the ovary. Pomes (pg. 11) are one type. Another is the strawberry (pg. 82); unlike a pome, however, the strawberry carries its seeds on the surface rather than in the center of the fruit.

Wild cucumber

Pepos are berry-like fruits with a very tough rind developed from the receptacle (in most fruits, the skin is developed from the ovary). Wild cucumber (pg. 46) is a pepo that is in this book; others which are not in this book are melons and gourds.

Red trillium

Capsules are dry, non-fleshy fruits that split at maturity to scatter their seeds. Most capsule fruits don't resemble anything we'd think of as fruit and are not included here; however, several, including trillium (pg. 88) have a large, fleshy capsule that looks like fruit, so they are included.

Common juniper

Cones are fruits that consist of scales (sporophylls) arranged in an overlapping or spiral fashion around a central core; seeds are developed between the scales. Common juniper (pg. 220), bald cypress (pg. 58) and eastern red cedar (pg. 236) are included in this book because their cones look berry-like.

HOW FRUITS ARE ARRANGED ON THE STEM

Fruits may grow singly on a stem, or in clusters. Locations also vary; fruits may grow at the ends of branches, along the branches, or in leaf axils. Here are a few of the common arrangements and locations.

Common chokecherry

A *raceme* is a cluster of fruit growing on a central stem; each fruit has its own stalk, and all stalks are of equal length. At left is a raceme of chokecherries. Racemes can also be branched, with each branch having a small raceme; this is called a *panicle*.

A rounded *umbrella-like cluster*, called an *umbel*, contains numerous fruit stalks that grow from a common point on the main fruiting stem. All stalks are the same length, so the cluster is rounded. The highbush cranberry shown at right is an example. Another type of umbrella-like cluster is called a *corymb*; in this arrangement, fruit stalks vary in length so that all fruits are aligned in a flat-topped cluster.

Highbush cranberry

The *leaf axil* is the point at which the leaf joins the stem; many fruits are attached at the axils. At right are glossy buckthorn fruits growing from the leaf axils.

Glossy buckthorn

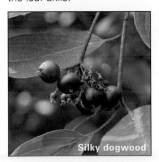
Silky dogwood

Fruits also grow at the end of the stem; at left is a cluster of silky dogwood fruits growing at the end of a stem.

LEAF FORM AND ARRANGEMENT

Leaves are one of the most important features to consider when attempting to identify a plant. Their shape, the way they attach to the plant, characteristics of the edge, and, of course, size and color must all be considered. Botanists use many terms to describe these things in exacting detail; this book does not reach so far, using terms geared to the layperson. Here is a brief overview of some of these terms.

Form and arrangement are the first characteristics to look at. The leaves of this honeysuckle are *simple*—a single leaf blade is attached to the stem of the plant. The leaf is narrowly oval, with a rounded base and pointed tip. Looking closer, we see that the leaf has a short *petiole*—the stemlet that attaches the leaf to the stem. The leaf is attached *oppositely*—directly across the stem from another leaf. Its edge

Amur honeysuckle

is *smooth*, not jagged or toothy. It is deep green and glossy above. The *midrib*—the long line that divides the leaf in two—is pale.

Gooseberry

Although the gooseberry leaves at left are also called simple, there's a lot more going on. They are *lobed*, meaning that each leaf, although whole and undivided, has several distinct sections, rather like a maple leaf. The petiole (stemlet) is much longer than that of the honeysuckle above. The leaves are arranged *alternately* on the stem, with some distance between the points where each leaf attaches to the stem. Leaf veins are noticeable but not prominent, and the midvein does not stand out as on the honeysuckle leaf. Leaf color is medium green above, and the surface is somewhat *rough*; leaf edges have *rounded teeth*, and the base is broad.

Black raspberry

Compound leaves look like a small stem with numerous leaves; the entire grouping is called a *blade*. Individual leaves on each blade are called *leaflets*. The blade is a true leaf, with a bud at its base; leaflets don't have buds. This black raspberry has three-part compound leaves—each blade has three leaflets, which have *sharply toothed edges*. Compound leaves can have a dozen or more leaflets on each blade. If they are arranged in a row along the blade stem, the blade is said to be *pinnately compound*; see mountain ash on pg. 78 for an example.

Some compound leaves are even more complicated, consisting of several compound leaves attached to the blade stem. The white baneberry pictured at right has *doubly compound* leaves: the blade has three compound leaves, each with five to seven leaflets. This plant has three doubly compound leaves: the one at the top, which also is bearing the fruiting stalk, and the two that are going off to the sides near the bottom of the photo.

White baneberry

Virginia creeper

The final type of compound leaf is called *palmately compound*. As shown by the leaves of this Virginia creeper, the leaflets all radiate from a central point, rather than growing on a blade stem.

Note that characteristics of the individual leaves shown here, other than leaf form, are not always as shown. For example, a simple leaf can have a long or short petiole (or no petiole); its edges may be pointed or smooth, and it may grow alternately.

LEAF ATTACHMENT

The previous pages showed some examples of leaf attachment; this page gives additional examples of those, as well as a few others that were not shown. Note that the text discusses the attachment of a leaf to the stem, but the same attachment styles could also apply to the attachment of a leaflet to a blade stem (on a compound leaf).

Crabapple

Many leaves are attached to the stem by a *petiole*, which can be defined as a leaf stemlet. Petioles can be long or short, smooth or hairy, round or flattened, and any color found in nature. The petioles on the crabapple leaves shown at left are long, smooth and greenish.

Some leaves are *sessile*—they attach directly to the stem. The false Solomon's seal shown below left is an example of this. *Perfoliate* leaves, like those of the large-flowered bellwort shown below right, have a base that extends slightly beyond the stem, giving the impression that the stem is growing up through the leaf.

False Solomon's seal

Large-flowered bellwort

Clasping leaves have no petiole (stemlet); the base of the leaf clasps, or slightly surrounds the stem, but does not extend beyond it. Smooth Solomon's seal, pictured at right, is an example of a clasping leaf.

Smooth Solomon's seal

Red trillium

Sometimes, three or more leaves grow from a common point of attachment. This style of leaf arrangement is called *whorled*, and is seen in the trillium photo at left.

To the botanist, leaf attachment and leaf arrangement are different discussions; for the layperson, the distinction is not important. The whorled example seems to cross into both categories.

LEAF SHAPES

Leaves and leaflets take numerous shapes; here are the most common. Note that leaves may taper on one or both ends, may have rounded or heart-shaped bases with pointed tips, or any number of combinations.

Lowbush blueberry

Oval leaves (sometimes called elliptic leaves) are the most familiar. At left are the oval leaves of blueberries.

Lance-shaped or sword-like leaves are long and slender; often, sides are almost parallel for much of the leaves' length. Below left are the lance-shaped leaves of starry false Solomon's seal.

Paddle-shaped leaves are narrow at the base, widening at or above the midpoint; they typically have a rounded tip. Below right are the paddle-shaped leaves of barberry.

Starry false Solomon's seal

Barberry

SAFETY AND PLANT IDENTIFICATION

If you are using this book to identify plants just for pleasure, that's great; hopefully, you will find what you're looking for and may even enjoy keeping a life list of fruits spotted. However, if you are planning to eat any of the fruits you identify, it is critical to follow good identification practices. Before sampling a plant's fruit, determine the plant's overall structure, its color, its leaf and stem arrangement, fruit appearance and characteristics. The photos and text in this book are as clear and concise as possible; however, they are not exhaustive. Sometimes, a plant looks slightly different than those photographed, and identification becomes a bit of a guessing game. It's prudent to consult more than one guidebook before consuming something you've foraged, and I strongly urge you to do so. The Helpful Resources on pgs. 318–319 will give you some sources that may be helpful. This extra effort is worth it; a mistake could cause illness or, in rare cases, death.

It's also important to note that individual reaction to foods varies; to some, the everyday peanut is a ballpark snack, while to others, it can cause life-threatening complications if ingested. Reactions to wild foods are not always well-documented or predictable; when you're eating an unfamiliar wild food, try just a small portion at first.

Also, remember that many wild foods are edible only at a certain stage of growth, or with certain special preparations. That information is beyond the scope of this book; however, the notes and information with each species account point out possible issues with the various fruits you may find. If the text has any indications that special preparations may be required, or that ripeness is critical to edibility, it is your responsibility to learn what is required to make certain your foraged fruits are edible and safe.

Some fruits are edible but not palatable; these are noted as "edible" in most cases, although in a few cases they are noted as "not edible" because they really aren't worth experimenting with. Others may cause

stomach upset or other relatively minor difficulties; these are noted as "not edible." Some, however, can kill if enough is ingested; and in a few cases, the amount is shockingly little. These plants are listed as "toxic" and contain the skull-and-crossbones symbol at left. Pay attention to this. It's not worth taking chances.

WHAT IS NOT INCLUDED IN THIS BOOK

In general, the fruits included in this book are those which most people would identify as fruits. Capsules such as those produced by poppies, maple-tree wings (samaras), and dry seeds such as sunflower seeds and wheat kernels, would not likely be considered a fruit, so are not in this book. Here are some other things which are not included.

Nuts

Nuts, such as these shagbark hickories, are large, dry fruits with hard seedcoats; they usually contain a single seed. Nuts are indehiscent, meaning that they remain closed when mature.

Legumes

Legumes are pods, often quite narrow, that contain pea-like or bean-like seeds. Legumes are dehiscent, meaning that they dry out and split open, releasing their seeds. Pods of American vetch are pictured at left.

Follicles

Follicles are dry, dehiscent fruits that dry out and split on one side to scatter their seeds. The fruit of a milkweed, a very common follicle, is pictured at left.

Galls

Galls are not a fruit, but rather a swelling in the stem of a plant caused by an insect The round bulge on this anemone could be easily mistaken for a fruit.

BE CERTAIN, BE SAFE: WILD GRAPES

Wild grapes are a prime wild edible; they're delicious and abundant. However, several other vining plants in our area have inedible or toxic fruits that appear somewhat similar to wild grapes. Fortunately, it's easy to distinguish between them if you pay attention when harvesting.

Below is a photo of riverbank grapes (pg. 190). On the next page, you'll find photos of some fruits that appear similar to these and other grapes (pgs. 190, 192, 254). Key identification points also help you distinguish between grapes and these other fruits. When harvesting wild grapes, always be certain you know which plant the fruit you're picking is growing on; Virginia creeper, for example, often intertwines with grape vines.

Riverbank grape

Canada moonseed (pg. 194)

Heartleaf peppervine (pg. 196)

Virginia creeper (pg. 214)

Smilax (pg. 262)

Cupseed (unripe; pg. 258)

LEAVES

Grape: Shallow to deep lobes, toothed edges

Canada moonseed: Three to seven shallow lobes, smooth edges

Peppervine: Heart-shaped, toothed edges

Virginia creeper: Palmately compound, coarsely toothed edges

Smilax: Heart-shaped or oval, typically smooth edges

Cupseed: Palmately lobed or heart-shaped, typically smooth edges

TENDRILS

Grape: Coiling tendrils

Canada moonseed: No tendrils

Peppervine: Branched tendrils

Virginia creeper: Sucker-foot tendrils

Smilax: Varies with species

Cupseed: No tendrils

FRUITS

Grape: Purplish to blackish, most types with blooms; cluster on sturdy stalk; up to six teardrop-shaped seeds (delicious)

Canada moonseed: Purplish with a bloom; loose clusters on thin stalk; single flat, crescent-shaped seed (toxic)

Peppervine: Multi-colored, speckled; wide, loose clusters (inedible)

Virginia creeper: Bluish-purple with a bloom; loose clusters on hot-pink stemlets (inedible)

Smilax: Bluish-black with a bloom; rounded cluster on stiff stalk (inedible)

Cupseed: Black or yellowish-black, no bloom; cluster on thin stalk (inedible)

RIPENING CALENDAR FOR EDIBLE FRUIT

	May	June
Gooseberry (pg. 48, 198, 266)		
Serviceberry (pg. 204)		
Black raspberry (pg. 262)		
Strawberry (pg. 82)		
Red, white mulberry (pg. 166)		
Blueberry (pg. 218, 224)		
Dewberry (pg. 124, 264)		
Black huckleberry (pg. 270)		
Sweet, sour, Mahaleb cherry (pg. 168)		
Red raspberry (pg. 124)		
Currant (pg. 128, 268)		
Crabapple (pg. 170)		
Fragrant sumac (pg. 126)		
Blackberry (pg. 272)		
Mock strawberry (pg. 90)		
Goji berry (pg. 130)		
Mayapple (pg. 60)		
Black cherry (pg. 300)		
Peach (pg. 76)		
Pin cherry (pg. 172)		
Purple-flowering raspberry (pg. 122)		
Common elderberry (pg. 200)		
Sand cherry (pg. 276)		
Bunchberry (pg. 92)		
Wild plum (pg. 174,176, 208)		
Yellow passionflower (pg. 216)		
Ground cherry (pg. 62)		
Common chokecherry (pg. 148)		
Hawthorn (pg. 180)		
Smooth, staghorn, winged sumac (pg. 182, 206)		

* *edible when green in color*

Timing may vary by several weeks from the southern to the northern part of our area, and also may vary from year to year depending on weather. Date ranges shown here are an average; fruits in any given area may ripen a week or two earlier—or later—than shown.

July	August	September	October	Winter

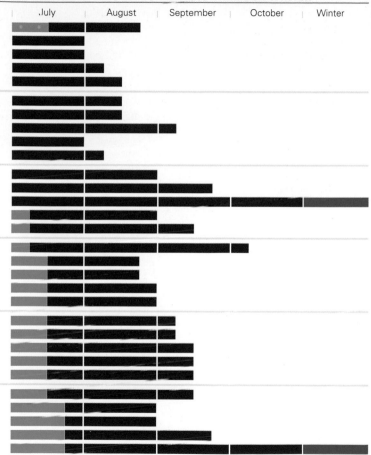

RIPENING CALENDAR FOR EDIBLE FRUIT (CONTINUED)

	May	June
Prickly pear (pg. 110)		
Bastard toadflax (pg. 34)		
Starry false Solomon's seal (pg. 102)		
Common pear (pg. 52)		
Maypop (pg. 44)		
Wild grapes, muscadine (pg. 190, 192, 254)		
Apple (pg. 170)		
Highbush cranberry (pg. 150)		
Common juniper (pg. 220)		
Russian olive (pg. 70)		
Callery pear (pg. 68)		
Hobblebush (pg. 288)		
Mountain ash (pg. 78)		
Partridge berry (pg. 98)		
Chokeberry (pg. 290)		
Yellow Mandarin (pg. 106)		
Deerberry (pg. 292)		
Withe-rod (pg. 226)		
Pawpaw (pg. 56)		
Autumn olive (pg. 154)		
Rose hip (pg. 134)		
Blackhaw, nannyberry (pg. 296)		
Japanese barberry (pg. 138)		
Northern spicebush (pg. 156)		
Hackberry, sugarberry (pg. 302)		
Blackgum (pg. 240)		
Farkleberry (pg. 292)		
Cranberry (pg. 118)		
Wintergreen (pg. 120)		
Persimmon (pg. 80)		

Timing may vary by several weeks from the southern to the northern part of our area, and also may vary from year to year depending on weather. Date ranges shown here are an average; fruits in any given area may ripen a week or two earlier—or later—than shown.

July	August	September	October	Winter

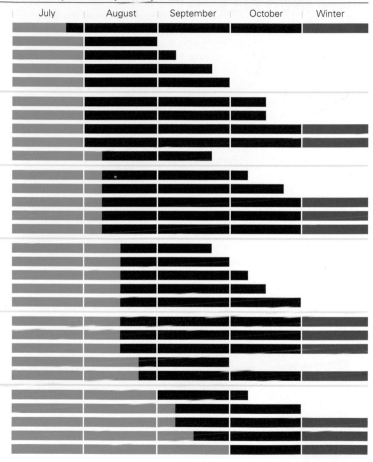

25

HOW TO USE THIS BOOK

1. When you find a plant with fruits, pay attention to **fruit color** first. Use the colored quarter-circles at the top corner of the left-hand pages to find the corresponding section.

SMALL
WOODY SHRUB

2. Next, identify the **form of the plant**: is it a tender leafy plant, a shrub (small or large?), a vine or a tree? Flip through the color section until you find the proper form, using the icon at the top of the page.

3. Look through the **photos** in this section and see if you find similar fruits. If you can't, look in the color sections before and after the section you're in; if you are looking at a red fruit, but don't see anything like it, go to the orange section or to the purple section. Color judgment is subjective, and individual specimens may vary slightly, so you may have to look for the fruit in several color sections.

Mountain ash

It's also possible that you've found unripe fruit, and since this book shows fruits in the ripe stage, you might not be looking in the right color section. Most fruits are green when immature, ripening to a

Black raspberry

different color; but some pass through several colors before fully ripening. Black raspberries (pg. 262), for example, start out green and ripen to black; in between they turn yellow, salmon-orange, bright red, and purplish-red. Other fruits undergo similar transformations. Once you find something that looks similar—even if it's the wrong color —proceed to the next step.

4. Look at the **range map** icon at the top of the page to determine whether the plant is found in your area. Use these range maps as an approximation, as there are few official sources of information pertaining to wild plants, and no resource is all-inclusive.

ALTERNATE LEAVES

5. When you find a photograph that appears similar to the fruit you've found (even if the color is not quite right), and the plant is the correct form, take a look at the **leaves** to see if they grow opposite one another on the stem, alternately on the stem, or in a whorl. This distinction is often the main key to properly identifying a plant.

6. Now read the full description, paying particular attention to any text that is in green; this color is used to point out key features that distinguish a plant from those with similar appearances. Also **study the "Compare"** section; here, you'll find information about plants that have similarities to the one pictured, along with page references for those which appear in this book. By following these references, you may sometimes find a photo showing the fruit you've found in a more ripened state; the description on that page will help you to identify the plant, even if you're looking at it in its unripe state.

SUMMER

7. To help determine when a fruit ripens, we've included a **season** icon at the top of the page. This will tell you the approximate season you're likely to find ripe berries or fruits and can help narrow down the possibilities when there are a number of look-alike fruits and berries.

8. Finally, the **thumb tab** at the top indicates whether a plant is toxic, not edible, edible, or delicious.

A species indicated as **toxic** has fruits that are highly poisonous and should not be eaten under any circumstances. The corresponding photo bears a skull and crossbones symbol for good reason: do not sample any part of a plant bearing this symbol. Species indicated as **not edible** bear fruit which, while not highly toxic, may cause sickness upon ingestion or have other negative side effects. Species indicated as **edible** bear fruits that are just that: edible. Some are bland but handy to know about as survival food, while others have a minor place in the forager's kitchen. Species indicated as **delicious** are the berries and fruits many people seek out. Blueberries, plums and choke-cherries are just a few of the many delicious wild fruits found in Indiana, Kentucky and Ohio. Unlike the fruits simply marked as edible, these are the best wild edibles the region has to offer.

Here's an example; follow along to see if you can identify this fruit.

The plant has fruit that is primarily red, and it is a large shrub (you can't see that in the photo above, but in the field, the form is obvious). Go to the red section of the book (starting on pg. 82), and flip to the beginning of the section that lists large shrubs (pg. 142).

LARGE
WOODY SHRUB

Twelve large shrubs (or large shrubs/small trees) are listed in the red section. Four of them (red elderberry, prickly ash, buttonbush and winged euonymus) can be eliminated, because the fruit doesn't look at all like this.

ALTERNATE
LEAVES

You notice that the leaves on this plant are alternate, spaced along the stem rather than across from one another. This eliminates bush honeysuckle and guelder rose/highbush cranberry. Six species remain as possibilities.

Examining the leaves more closely, you note that they have fine teeth. This eliminates autumn olive and northern spicebush, whose leaves have smooth edges. You can also eliminate American holly because its leaves have spine-tipped points.

Five choices remain: common chokecherry (pg. 148); winterberry, catberry and possumhaw (pg. 152); and Carolina buckthorn (pg. 162). First,

double-check the range maps for the species. You're in southern Ohio; you note that catberry and possumhaw are not in your region, so they are eliminated. Chokecherry, winterberry and Carolina buckthorn remain possibilities. The descriptions for winterberry and Carolina buckthorn mention that the fruits grow from leaf axils, but the fruits on your plant are in a hanging cluster. Studying the text on the chokecherry page, it seems likely that you've found a chokecherry.

To confirm your identification, study the "Compare" text on pg. 148 to see what other plants resemble this one. Looking at the photos of black cherry (pg. 300) and pin cherry (pg. 172), you see that although the fruit is similar, those plants have leaves that are much narrower. In addition, your plant doesn't have any hairs on the midrib underneath, so it's not a black cherry, and the fruit on your plant is growing in a hanging cluster (a raceme) so it's not a pin cherry. The leaves do look like those of the serviceberry (pg. 204), but the fruit is not similar.

You've found a common chokecherry, a delicious wild edible fruit.

Once you've identified your wild fruit or berry, check the bottom of the page, as we've included a reference to our companion book, *Cooking with Wild Berries & Fruits of Indiana, Kentucky and Ohio*, which includes delicious recipes, handy tips, and many different ways to put your newly found edible fruits and berries to use.

SMALL
WOODY SHRUB

ALTERNATE
COMPOUND
LEAVES

EARLY TO
MID SUMMER

Common Name

Scientific name

HABITAT: General environment in which the plant is typically found in our area, including light and moisture requirements

GROWTH: The growth form of the plant in our area, ranging from small, tender plants, to vines, to small or large shrubs, to trees

LEAVES: Description of the plant's leaves, including leaf style and shape, arrangement on the plant, attachment to the main stem, and color of the leaves

FRUIT: Description of the fruit, including type (berry, pome, drupe or other), color, arrangement, appearance and edibility information

SEASON: When the plant bears ripe fruit in our area

COMPARE: Plants or fruits with similar attributes, including characteristics that differentiate them

NOTES: Interesting facts about the plant, including harvesting tips for edible plants, notes on other parts of the plant that may be edible, historical or modern-day medicinal uses, and miscellaneous tips and facts

TENDER
LEAFY PLANT

BASAL GROWTH
WITH PAIRED
LEAVES ON TOP

LATE SPRING
TO SUMMER

Celandine Poppy
–OR– Wood Poppy

Stylophorum diphyllum

HABITAT: Rich, moist deciduous woodlands and along stream edges; also found at the foot of bluffs and at the bottoms of ravines. It prefers shade, but will tolerate dappled sun. Celandine poppy often forms large colonies.

GROWTH: This native wildflower is a tender perennial, 12 to 18 inches in height. A hairy stem arises from a whorl of leaves at the base; paired leaves grow at the end of the stem. One to four yellow flowers, each with four petals, grow on long, hairy stemlets at the end of the main stem.

LEAVES: Large, multi-lobed leaves are up to 6 inches long and almost as wide. Each leaf has five to seven lobes, each with smaller lobes along the edges. The two lobes closest to the stem are slightly separated from the group of lobes at the end of the leaf. Leaves are blue-green above and silvery below.

FRUIT: A football-shaped, densely hairy capsule, 1 to 1½ inches long, replaces each flower. Capsules typically droop from the stemlets. Eventually, each capsule splits into 4 parts, dispersing the seeds. The plant also reproduces through rhizomes (underground root-bearing stems). The plant is listed as poisonous, and no part should be eaten.

SEASON: Bright yellow flowers appear in early spring, followed by the fruiting capsule which is present from late spring through midsummer.

COMPARE: Greater celandine (*Chelidonium majus*) is an introduced plant with similar leaves and flowers, but the fruits resemble green beans and the leaves are not as deeply lobed. Several poppy species (*Papaver* spp.) have also escaped cultivation and are found occasionally in our area; the fruiting capsules are similar, but the leaves are much smaller and grow alternately along the length of the stem.

NOTES: Stems contain a yellow sap that was once used as a dye. Ointment made from the plant has been used to heal skin lesions and burns.

green = key identification feature

Flower

TENDER
LEAFY PLANT

ALTERNATE
LEAVES

MID TO
LATE SUMMER

Bastard Toadflax
Comandra umbellata

HABITAT: Meadows, grasslands, prairies, woodland edges, and dry, open woods; occasionally found in mixed evergreen forests. It requires plenty of sunlight and good drainage.

GROWTH: This small, erect native perennial is typically 4 to 8 inches high, but can reach 16 inches; it often grows in large colonies. Stems are light green and smooth, and woody near the base. Although it is able to photosynthesize, it also uses suckers (shoots) to attach itself to the roots of other plants, stealing water and nutrients from them.

LEAVES: The thick, alternate leaves are 1 to 2 inches long and about one-quarter as wide. They are attached directly to the stem or by a very short petiole (stemlet). Leaves are light grayish-green and smooth, with smooth edges that may appear slightly turned under. Some leaf tips may have a slight reddish tinge. The midvein is prominent on the underside of the leaf.

FRUIT: Green drupes about ¼ inch across, with a **long, reddish crown** at the end; the fruits seem large in proportion to the plant. Fruits grow on long stemlets in clusters at the end of the main stem. The fruits are sweet when young, but have thin flesh with a slightly oily texture. They make a decent trailside nibble, but are not worth seeking out. Later in the season, the fruits turn brown and become unappetizing.

SEASON: Bastard toadflax produces white flowers in late spring through midsummer; fruits ripen in mid to late summer.

COMPARE: The leaves and growth habit of bastard toadflax resemble true toadflax (*Linaria* spp.), but *Linaria* don't produce drupes.

NOTES: The flower stamens have small hairs at their bases, giving the plant its species name, *Comandra* (a combination of the Greek words for "hair" and "man"). *Umbellata* refers to the flat-topped, umbrella-like flower clusters. Comandra is an alternate common name for bastard toadflax.

green = key identification feature

TOXIC

TENDER
LEAFY PLANT

ALTERNATE
LEAVES

SUMMER
THROUGH FALL

Thorn apple

Sacred jimsonweed
*see below

Jimsonweed

Datura spp.

HABITAT: Two jimsonweed species appear in our region: *Datura stramonium*, the common variety which is also called thorn apple; and *D. wrightii*, sacred jimsonweed (pictured at right). Both are found in sunny pastures, waste ground, agricultural areas, and alongside rural roads.

GROWTH: An erect annual plant, generally 2 to 4 feet tall and bushy, with smooth, **purplish stems that fork repeatedly**. Each fork bears a white or pale lavender flower shaped like a deep, angular funnel with well-defined edges and sharp tips. The flowers have a pleasant scent, but all other parts of the plant have a foul odor, especially when crushed.

LEAVES: Alternate, dark green on top, lighter underneath, generally 4 to 6 inches long. Thorn-apple leaves have **pointed, irregular teeth and several lobes**; they resemble an elongated maple or red-oak leaf. Sacred jimsonweed leaves typically have **wavy edges and shallow or non-existent lobes**.

FRUIT: Thorn-apple fruit is egg-shaped, about 2 inches long, growing **upright** from the fork of the stems. Fruit of sacred jimsonweed is more globe-like, up to 1½ inches, growing from the fork on a **drooping stem-let**. Fruits of both species are **covered in spiny prickles**. Fruits are green when young, eventually turning brown and splitting to scatter seeds.

SEASON: Jimsonweed flowers throughout summer and into fall; fruits develop from the flower remnants throughout the season.

COMPARE: Bluestem pricklypoppy (*Argemone albiflora*), which in our area is found occasionally in Ohio and Kentucky, has an egg-shaped spiny fruit growing upright on the stem, but leaves are prickly with multiple lobes; it is much less bushy.

NOTES: Thorn apple is non-native; it was noted in Jamestown, Virginia, during colonial days. Although sacred jimsonweed is a native plant, both it and thorn apple are considered pests in agricultural areas; cattle can be poisoned if they graze on the plants. Both contain scopolamine, atropine and hyoscyamine, powerful alkaloids that cause hallucinations, various physical difficulties, and, occasionally, death.

green = key identification feature   *specific IN locations not available

TENDER
LEAFY PLANT

ALTERNATE
LEAVES

LATE
SUMMER

Apple-of-Peru –OR– Shoo-fly   *Nicandra physalodes*

HABITAT: This non-native plant has escaped from gardens, and is found in disturbed areas, fields and waste ground, where it may spread and become weedy in appearance. It grows best in full to partial sun.

GROWTH: A branched, upright annual that may be up to 5 feet in height, although it is typically shorter; when large, it is usually very leafy. The main stem is slightly ridged, and may have a purplish cast. Pale purple flowers grow at the ends of stems that originate in the leaf axils; the calyx (the green petal-like structure at the base of the flower) is **sharply angled, net-veined and mottled with purple**. After flowering, the flower remnant turns downward and the calyx closes around it; a round berry forms inside the loose, husk-like calyx. Over time, both the calyx and the berry wither and turn brown, breaking open to release the seeds.

LEAVES: Oval leaves with a pointed tip, tapered base and large, irregular teeth grow alternately on grooved petioles (stemlets); leaves are 3 to 8 inches long and half as wide. They are medium-green on top, and often have a scattering of **tiny black dots**; undersides are paler.

FRUIT: A round, many-seeded berry, ½ inch across, grows inside the papery husk, which has **five sharply angled edges that end in pointed tips at the base**. The berry is green during development, turning brown and withering away on maturity. It is often regarded as mildly toxic, and should not be eaten.

SEASON: Apple-of-Peru flowers in mid to late summer; green fruits develop in late summer, withering to brown in fall.

COMPARE: Ground cherries (pg. 62) have similar round berries inside papery husks, but their husks are not as sharply angled as those of apple-of-Peru, and they lack the pointed tips at the base; also, ground cherry husks are not mottled with purple.

NOTES: The flowers last a single day before withering; they are reputed to repel insects.

green = key identification feature

Berry inside calyx

TENDER PLANT
(SUBSHRUB)

BASAL
GROWTH

MID TO
LATE SUMMER

* see below

Yucca –OR– **Adam's Needle**

Yucca filamentosa

HABITAT: Sandy, sunny areas including prairies, waste ground, roadsides, open woods, and railroad beds. Adam's needle is native to the southeastern United States, and is grown in our area as a showy garden specimen; it has escaped cultivation and is found occasionally in the wild in our area. Some texts refer to this plant as *Y. smalliana,* which is more commonly an alternate name for weak-leaf yucca (*Y. flaccida*).

GROWTH: Adam's needle appears to be a tender plant, but is actually a perennial subshrub. The **spiky, evergreen leaves grow in a tight cluster,** and the thick flowering stalk arises from the center of the leaves. The flowering stalk has **multiple branches** and may be up to 6 feet in height.

LEAVES: Stiff, sword-shaped leaves grow in a basal form. Leaves are slightly rough in texture, with a blue-green color; they are up to 2½ feet long, with bases up to 2 inches wide. Tips are sharply pointed; leaf edges are smooth but the leaves often have **whitish thread-like fibers** curling away from the edges.

FRUIT: The **lumpy, rounded green fruit** has two distinct lobes; it is up to 2½ inches long and half as wide. In fall, the pod darkens and splits into three parts to release its seeds. The pods are generally regarded as inedible, although some people steam *immature* pods to eat as a vegetable.

SEASON: Showy white flowers, which are pleasantly fragrant, bloom in late spring through midsummer (depending on location); the green seed pods are formed in mid to late summer.

COMPARE: Yucca leaves resemble the leaves of iris plants (*Iris* spp.), a common wildflower. However, iris flowers grow on a single stalk rather than a multi-branched flowering stalk like yucca, and the fruit pod lacks the distinct lobes. Iris also prefers wetter habitat.

NOTES: In spring, before the flowers develop, the central stalk can be cooked and eaten like asparagus. The flowers may be breaded and fried; they are also edible raw, but may have an unpleasant aftertaste.

green = key identification feature   *specific OH locations not available

Adam's needle fruit

Adam's needle plant in flower

WOODY VINE

ALTERNATE COMPOUND LEAVES

SUMMER

Eastern Poison Ivy

Toxicodendron radicans

HABITAT: This native woody vine grows throughout most of our area, and is found in a variety of habitats. It thrives in moist areas with moderate sun such as road ditches, open woodlands, fencelines, swampy areas and streambanks, but it may also be found in agricultural fields, sandy areas and disturbed sites.

GROWTH: A woody perennial vine that climbs trees, fences, posts and anything else it encounters, attaching itself to the supporting structure with **thick, hairy stems** (the hairs are actually aerial roots). Stems are reddish to gray. Eastern poison ivy may also grow as a shrub, or even a ground-hugging plant; it also hybridizes with western poison ivy (*T. rydbergii,* pg. 306), a low-growing form.

LEAVES: Three-part leaves grow on the ends of long, pale green petioles (stemlets) attached alternately to the main stem. The stemlet of the middle leaflet is **longer than those of the side leaflets.** Leaves of eastern poison ivy are often up to 8 inches long, much larger than those of western poison ivy. Edges have large, **irregular teeth.** Leaves turn yellow to reddish in fall, often with a blotchy appearance.

FRUIT: The round, **ridged** berries are ⅛ to ³⁄₁₆ inch across and green when immature, ripening to whitish. Berries of eastern poison ivy grow from leaf axils in loose clusters; the **clusters are usually large and abundant.** Berries, and all other parts of the plant, are toxic and may cause a painful rash if touched.

SEASON: Green berries are present much of the summer, ripening to white in the fall.

COMPARE: Western poison ivy is a low-growing plant, with smaller leaves and fewer berries. Both are toxic.

NOTES: Eastern poison ivy is common throughout most of our region. It is included here, in the green section of the book, because its abundant green berries are prominent most of the summer, and pose a threat to inquisitive children. See pg. 306 for more information on poison ivy.

green = key identification feature

Aerial roots on stem

TENDER VINE

ALTERNATE LEAVES

LATE SUMMER THROUGH FALL

Passionflower –or– Maypop

Passiflora incarnata

HABITAT: This native vine is found in sunny locations such as field edges, fencerows, unmowed pastures, railroad embankments, streambanks, waste ground and ditches; it prefers sandy soil and full sun.

GROWTH: A non-woody vine up to 30 feet long, passionflower uses **tendrils** to twine itself around other plants, fences and buildings, often reaching a height of 10 feet or more; if a supporting structure is not present, it will sprawl along the ground. It spreads very aggressively. Stems are smooth or slightly hairy. Distinctive **purple, frilly flowers**, 2 to 3 inches across, grow throughout the summer from the leaf axils.

LEAVES: Palmately lobed leaves with three divisions (occasionally five) grow alternately on the vine on medium-length petioles (stemlets); two **sticky tendrils** are present where the leaf attaches to the petiole. Leaves are 3 to 6 inches across with pointed tips and finely toothed edges. The top surface is dark green and smooth; the underside is paler.

FRUIT: Egg-shaped berries, 2 to 3 inches long, are green and smooth at first, becoming yellowish and wrinkly with age. When cut open, the fruit reveals a **thick, spongy white rind filled with seeds, each surrounded by translucent, gel-like pulp.** The seedy pulp is edible, with a sweet-tart flavor; it is often juiced, but can be eaten raw or cooked.

SEASON: Flowers are present from spring through summer; fruits ripen from late summer through early fall.

COMPARE: Yellow passionflower (pg. 216) is a similar vine, but its leaves are less deeply lobed; its flowers are yellow, and ripe fruits are very small and bluish.

NOTES: Passionflower fruits burst with a "pop" when stepped on, possibly accounting for the common name. Ripe maypops may be green or yellowish, but they are heavier than underripe fruit of the same size (Sam Thayer). Underripe maypops can be left on a counter to ripen, but flavor is best when vine-ripened. Herbalists prepare a sedative from the leaves; the fruits may have a sedative effect when eaten.

green = key identification feature

Cut-open maypop

TENDER
VINE

ALTERNATE
LEAVES

LATE SUMMER
THROUGH FALL

Wild Cucumber
–OR– **Balsam Apple**

Echinocystis lobata

HABITAT: Streambanks, moist thickets and woods, roadsides, swamp edges. Generally found in sunny locations.

GROWTH: A native, non-woody vining plant with coiled tendrils; nodes are sometimes hairy. Grows rapidly, and can reach 25 feet in length.

LEAVES: Alternating leaves, somewhat resembling maple leaves, grow on long petioles (stemlets); each typically has five distinct triangular lobes, but may have as few as three or as many as seven lobes.

FRUIT: A pulpy green berry-like fruit with a firm skin (called a *pepo*), 1 to 2 inches long, roughly egg-shaped, sometimes with blunt ends, grows on a short stalk from the leaf node. The fruit has supple, spiny prickles overall. Eventually the fruit dries out and turns brown, splitting open at the end to disperse its four seeds. The fruit is inedible.

SEASON: Wild cucumber blooms in mid to late summer, producing a profusion of lacy white flowers that may blanket the surrounding vegetation; fruits are present from late summer through fall.

COMPARE: Wild grapes (pgs. 190, 192, 254) are vining plants with similar leaves, but their fruits grow in clusters like the familiar commercial grape. Guadeloupe cucumber (*Melothria pendula*) has similar leaves and growth form, but its fruits are small, smooth, tough-skinned pepos that lack prickles; in our area, it is found occasionally in Kentucky and southern Indiana. Bur cucumber (*Sicyos angulatus*), found scattered throughout our area, has a spiny green fruit that is not egg-shaped but rather has many points, looking something like a small, prickly, three-dimensional star ornament.

NOTES: The roots of wild cucumber have been used medicinally to treat ailments including headache, stomach problems, rheumatism and even love-sickness. According to *Native American Ethnobotany* (Daniel E. Moerman; Timber Press), the seeds were used as beads by American Indian peoples.

green = key identification feature

SMALL
WOODY SHRUB

ALTERNATE
LEAVES

LATE SPRING
TO SUMMER

* see below

Gooseberries (green stage)

Ribes spp.

HABITAT: Three native gooseberry species are found in our area: Missouri (*Ribes missouriense*), prickly or pasture (*R. cynosbati*), and smooth or swamp (*R. hirtellum,* which does not grow in Kentucky). Gooseberries inhabit thickets and tangled areas, scrubby shelterbelts, rocky areas, and rich, moist woods, especially those along rivers or ponds.

GROWTH: An arching shrub about 3 feet high. Missouri and prickly gooseberry stems have scattered small bristles on young and mature stems. Mature stems of smooth gooseberries have small hairs but no bristles; young stems have scattered small prickles. Leaf nodes of all three have one to three sharp thorns.

LEAVES: Attached alternately to the stem by a petiole (stemlet). Each leaf has three to five distinct lobes, resembling a rounded maple leaf. Leaf undersides are slightly hairy on smooth and Missouri gooseberries; prickly gooseberry leaves have more hairs on the undersides.

FRUIT: The ¼- to ½-inch round berry grows singly or in clusters of two or three. Prickly gooseberry fruits have soft prickles, either overall or around the half of the fruit closest to the stem; fruits of the others are smooth. All have distinct stripes that run longitudinally; a stiff flower remnant, called a pigtail, is present at the end of the berry. Gooseberries are green when young, ripening to red, purple or black.

SEASON: Fruit is green but edible in late spring through midsummer.

COMPARE: Currant shrubs (pgs. 128, 268) resemble gooseberry shrubs, but fruits are borne in racemes (long clusters of multiple fruits). Horse nettle (pg. 64) bears **toxic** green berries on prickly stems, but it is a shorter plant, not a shrub, with leaves that resemble oak, not maple.

NOTES: Green gooseberries are rich in pectin, and are used primarily for jam, jelly and pie. Taste a few before harvesting; they will be sour, but if they are too astringent, let them mature a bit longer before picking. When the fruits ripen (pgs. 198, 266), they are excellent in baked desserts, sauces and other dishes.

green = key identification feature   *combined range

Missouri gooseberry

Prickly gooseberry

TREE

OPPOSITE
LEAVES

MID TO
LATE SUMMER

Princess Tree

Paulownia tomentosa

HABITAT: This non-native tree has escaped cultivation, and is increasingly found in the wild, where it is becoming a weedy, invasive tree. It prefers areas with deep, moist, well-drained soil, but is tolerant of drought and pollution; it is found in woodland edges and disturbed forests, along railroad beds and streambanks, and on rocky slopes.

GROWTH: This large tree can grow as much as 12 feet in a season, and can reach a height of 50 feet, with equal spread; wild specimens tend to be smaller. Bark is grayish-brown with narrow fissures; twigs are brown or green with numerous lenticels (breathing pores). In spring, it produces hundreds of pale lavender flowers before the leaves develop, making a striking display.

LEAVES: Heart-shaped leaves, **as much as 12 inches long** and about two-thirds as wide, grow oppositely on long, smooth petioles (stemlets). Some trees have leaves with several sharply pointed lobes on the sides, while others have smooth edges with no lobes. Leaves are dark green on top and paler below, and lightly fuzzy or rough on both sides; edges are untoothed. Veins are prominent on the undersides.

FRUIT: The fruit, a dry capsule, looks a bit like an **elongated green acorn with a loose, frilly brown cap.** When fully developed, it is 1½ to 2 inches long and half as wide, with a broad top and a pointed tip; the hard shell is green, with a **rough, sticky texture.** The fruit is not edible.

SEASON: Developed green fruits are present in mid to late summer; in fall, they turn brown and split open, spilling over 1,000 seeds per fruit. Small **brown flower buds** follow and are present through winter.

COMPARE: Catalpa trees (*Catalpa* spp.) somewhat resemble princess trees, but catalpa fruits are long, thin, hanging pods.

NOTES: Paulownia wood is prized for carving in China and Japan. Some sources say that in its native China, a princess tree is planted when a baby girl is born. The tree matures with the child; when she reaches the age of marriage, its wood is used to carve items for her dowry.

green = key identification feature

TREE

ALTERNATE LEAVES

MID TO LATE SUMMER

Common Pear

Pyrus communis

HABITAT: This is the common orchard pear, which has escaped cultivation and is found in scattered spots in the wild. Pears may be "planted" by anglers, hunters or picnickers who throw out a core after eating a commercial pear, so they are found near boat launches, parks and hiking trails. Pears do best in sunny areas with rich, moist, well-drained soil.

GROWTH: A medium to large tree, with a straight trunk and an open, spreading crown. Unlike orchard pears, which are grafted onto shorter stock to make picking easy, wild pears grow from seed, and tend to be taller than their domestic cousins. The trunk has furrowed grayish bark. Branches are reddish-brown to grayish; most are smooth, with visible gray lenticels (breathing pores), but side branches often have wrinkled bark or are knobby-looking. Pear trees have no thorns.

LEAVES: Glossy, thick, leathery leaves, up to 4 inches long and two-thirds as wide, grow alternately or in clusters on long yellowish-green petioles (stemlets). Leaves have pointed tips and are broadest near the base or below the midpoint; they often fold in slightly along the midline. Edges are finely serrated, and may appear wavy.

FRUIT: A greenish to yellowish pome, generally 1 to 2 inches across; the skin is rough, with fine brown patches or tiny dots. Pears grow on a thick stemlet and have a crown on the bottom. Unlike commercial pears, wild pears have little or no neck; they often grow with the crown end up, looking like a large, rough-skinned crabapple. Wild pears are generally firmer than domestic pears, but taste similar. There are no toxic look-alikes that have a crown on the bottom.

SEASON: Wild pears ripen in mid to late summer.

COMPARE: Crabapples (pg. 170) are similar trees, but leaves taper at both ends, and are thinner and rougher than pear leaves; branches have thorns. Callery pears (pg. 68) have smaller fruits that are bronze in color.

NOTES: Wild pears may fall off the tree before fully ripe, but will ripen if left on the countertop for a few days.

green = key identification feature

TREE

ALTERNATE
LEAVES

LATE SUMMER
TO EARLY FALL

Osage Orange
–OR– Hedge Apple

Maclura pomifera

HABITAT: Open sunny areas and rich bottomlands are prime habitat; also found in pastures, along fencerows, and occasionally along riverbanks.

GROWTH: A deciduous tree, up to 40 feet high with approximately equal width. Osage orange has many branches, and the foliage is dense, giving the appearance of a very solid tree. The trunk has brown bark with strong vertical fissures and orange patches. Only female trees bear fruit, and not until they are about 10 years old.

LEAVES: Bright green oblong leaves, 3 to 7 inches long, grow alternately on the stems. Leaves are smooth and glossy, with a rounded base and sharply pointed tip; although the edges are smooth, the leaves tend to curl upwards along the edges and may appear wavy. Half-inch-long thorns grow at leaf nodules. If a leaf or thorn is pulled off, milky sap will appear on the stem (careful; the sap may irritate the skin).

FRUIT: The pebbly-textured, leathery sphere, 4 to 6 inches across, consists of a pithy core surrounded by abundant small seeds. The fruit is light green with fine hairs when immature, ripening to hairless yellowish-green with a mild orange scent. Osage orange fruit is generally regarded as mildly toxic; sap from the fruit can cause skin irritation.

SEASON: Osage orange blooms in early summer; the large, round fruit grows throughout summer, ripening in late summer to early fall.

COMPARE: Nothing in our area resembles the fruit of the Osage orange.

NOTES: Osage orange is named after the Osage, an American Indian tribe that inhabited the tree's native range in Oklahoma and portions of the surrounding states. It is not native to our area, having been introduced as a hedge plant. Some people place Osage orange fruits around the foundation of the house, in the basement or near windows and doors to repel insects. The fruit also provides food for squirrels that shred it and strip the slimy husk off the seeds before eating them.

green = key identification feature

Mature fruit
and thorns

TREE

ALTERNATE
LEAVES

LATE SUMMER
TO EARLY FALL

Pawpaw
Asimina triloba

HABITAT: Areas with deep, rich soil including bottomlands, stream and river-banks, floodplains, ravines and ditches. Pawpaw prefers sun, but also grows in shady areas; it produces the most fruit in sunny areas.

GROWTH: This native tree can attain heights up to 40 feet, but is usually much shorter; it may appear shrub-like. It often grows in a "patch" or thicket, with larger central trees towering over the smaller surrounding upstarts. Bark is smooth and light brown, often with light-colored splotches; it has numerous small, wart-like lenticels (breathing pores). Twigs are downy when young, becoming smooth as they mature.

LEAVES: Thick, bright green leaves grow alternately on short petioles (stemlets); they tend to cluster towards the ends of the branches. Leaves are oblong, with tapered bases and a pointed tip; they are up to 11 inches long and about one-third as wide, broadest above the midpoint. They have smooth edges and numerous prominent veins.

FRUIT: Green, smooth-skinned fruits grow singly or in clusters on short, thick stemlets along the branches. Fruits are typically oblong and some-what irregularly shaped; they are 2 to 6 inches long. Ripe fruits are softer to the touch, and are often pale yellowish-green with brown flecks. The interior of the ripe fruit is creamy yellow, with 8 to 13 large, flat, oval inedible seeds. The fruit is a prime edible, tasting similar to a banana with pineapple and apricot overtones (it is often called Indiana banana). It can be eaten raw, or used in baked goods. It may cause stomach upset or intestinal problems in some people. There are no toxic look-alikes.

SEASON: Pawpaw fruits are present much of the summer, but don't ripen until late summer to early fall.

COMPARE: A smaller form, the dwarf or small-flowered pawpaw (*A. parviflora*) grows in the southeast but not in our area.

NOTES: Pawpaw is the State Native Fruit of Ohio and is celebrated annually at the Ohio Pawpaw Festival in Albany, Ohio. Kentucky State University is home to the only full-time pawpaw research facility in the world.

green = key identification feature

Leaves

TREE

ALTERNATE
LEAVES

LATE SUMMER
TO EARLY FALL

* see below

Bald Cypress

Taxodium distichum

HABITAT: Bald cypress is native to the southeast; it grows naturally in areas that are wet throughout much of the year, although it can be grown as a landscape tree in drier locations. In our area, it is found in the wild along streams and rivers, in swamps, on lake margins, or in low areas with moving water. It requires a fair amount of sun, and grows best in acidic soil.

GROWTH: A large, somewhat open tree with **deciduous needle-like leaves**, bald cypress is often over 100 feet in height. Bark is reddish-brown to grayish, with long, flat ridges; it peels off in thin vertical strips. Trees growing in locations that are usually flooded have a **flared, swollen base** up to 6 feet across; they also have unusual "knees," which are **pyramid- or cone-shaped root projections** that grow around the base of the tree, above the normal water level. It is thought that the knees and swollen base help stabilize the tree in loose, swampy soil.

LEAVES: Flat, soft, needle-like leaves, ½ to ¾ inch long, grow alternately on thin, tender twigs that grow at right angles from the woody branches. The leaf-covered twigs droop as they mature over summer. Leaves turn copper-colored to brown in fall; twigs drop off in late fall or early winter.

FRUIT: Leathery round cones, ¾ to 1¼ inches across, are **knobby and green** when young; as they mature, they become wrinkly and tannish-green or gray with green furrows. Fully mature cones are brown and woody, but unlike pinecones, they do not open up; rather, the flake-like scales simply fall away as the cone disintegrates. The cones are not edible.

SEASON: Cones are immature in early summer, maturing in late summer to early fall; they usually remain on the trees through early winter.

COMPARE: Pond cypress (*T. ascendens*) is a similar, related tree, but its leaves are awl-like and overlapping; it is not found in our area in the wild, occurring naturally only in the coastal southeastern states.

NOTES: The seeds are eaten by squirrels and many birds, including wood ducks and wild turkeys; eagles, herons and other large birds nest in the upper branches. Bald cypress is listed as threatened in Indiana.

green = key identification feature   *specific OH locations not available

Maturing cones

TENDER
LEAFY PLANT

OPPOSITE
LEAVES

MID TO LATE
SUMMER

Mayapple –OR– Mandrake

Podophyllum peltatum

HABITAT: Rich, somewhat shaded woodlands with loamy soil. This native plant grows in sun or shade, but requires moderate sun to produce fruit.

GROWTH: A smooth green stem grows from a rhizome (underground root-bearing stem) to a height of 12 to 18 inches; a large palmately lobed leaf grows at the top of the stem. Some plants have a forked stem, with a large leaf on top of each fork; only forked plants will flower and produce fruit. Mayapples usually grow in large colonies.

LEAVES: Each deep green, palmately lobed leaf is 8 to 10 inches wide and has five to nine lobes with toothy edges; the overall outline is a circle. Plants with a single stem have one leaf, while those with a forked stem have two. A colony of mayapple plants resembles a miniature woodland café, with the leaves serving as patio umbrellas.

FRUIT: In spring, a single flower grows on a long stemlet from the fork in the stem. An egg-shaped green berry appears after the flower, and matures slowly over the summer; full-sized berries can be up to 2 inches long. When the leaves start dying, the plant often falls to the ground with the unripe green fruit still attached; foragers typically gather the fruit at that time and let it ripen to yellow on the countertop. Fully ripe berries are edible raw but are usually cooked or juiced; they have a lemony, tropical taste, and numerous small seeds like those of cantaloupe. Caution is essential because *seeds, unripe berries and all other parts of the plant are toxic*. As with all wild edibles, eat only a small portion until you are sure you won't have an adverse reaction. Before picking or eating any mayapples, it's best to get the guidance of a forager who is experienced in judging ripeness of the fruit.

SEASON: Berries ripen to yellow from mid to late summer.

COMPARE: Goldenseal (pg. 86) has a has a similar growth habit, with a forked stem topped by a large leaf; however, the fruits are dissimilar.

NOTES: The rhizome is extremely toxic, but is used medicinally to treat genital warts; studies suggest it may also have anti-cancer properties.

green = key identification feature

Unripe mayapple berry on plant (all parts of the plant are toxic at this stage)

Ripe mayapple berry

TENDER
LEAFY PLANT

ALTERNATE
LEAVES

MID TO
LATE SUMMER

* see below

Ground Cherries

Physalis spp.

HABITAT: Fields, slopes, rocky areas and waste ground; often found along fences, streams and railroad grades. They are native to our area.

GROWTH: A very leafy plant, 1 to 4 feet in height. Depending on variety, it grows as a perennial from **rhizomes** (underground root-bearing stems), or as an annual from a **taproot**. In our area, perennials include the clammy (*Physalis heterophylla*), smooth (*P. longifolia*) and Virginia (*P. virginiana*) ground cherry; annuals include downy (*P. pubescens*), strawberry-tomato (*P. grisea*) and cutleaf (*P. angulata*) ground cherry.

LEAVES: Alternate, on short to medium petioles (stemlets). Leaf shapes are highly variable; leaves of some species have large, irregular teeth, but others are smooth-edged or slightly wavy.

FRUIT: A round, many-seeded berry, ½ to ¾ inch across, is enclosed in a **ribbed husk** that hangs from a leaf axil or stem fork; husks of most species have **10 equally spaced ribs** that may be subtle. Berries of the listed species are yellow to orangish when ripe. *Unripe berries and all other parts of the plant, including the papery husk, are toxic.*

SEASON: **Yellow** bell-shaped flowers, generally with dark spots inside the base, are present all summer; the berries ripen in mid to late summer.

COMPARE: Several non-native husk fruits may be found in our area as escapees from cultivation. Tomatillo (*P. philadelphica*) has edible 1-inch-wide berries that fill the husk completely. The inedible Chinese lantern (*P. alkekengi*) has an orange husk. Apple-of-Peru (pg. 38) has an inedible green berry, and its purple-spotted husk has very sharply angled edges.

NOTES: Key features help identify individual species. Clammy ground cherry has sticky hairs overall; leaves are wide with large, rounded teeth. Smooth and Virginia have narrow leaves that often lack teeth; those of smooth ground cherry often have an asymmetrical base, and the stem is grooved. Downy and strawberry-tomato husks have five sharply distinct ribs; downy have heart-shaped leaves, while those of strawberry-tomato are narrower. Cutleaf has dark veins on the husk.

green = key identification feature   *combined range

Ripe ground cherries

Clammy
ground cherry

Smooth
ground cherry

Husks shown contain
unripe green berries
(all parts of the plant
are toxic at this stage)

TENDER
LEAFY PLANT

ALTERNATE
LEAVES

SUMMER
THROUGH FALL

* see below

Horse Nettles

Solanum spp.

HABITAT: Two types of horse nettle are native to our area: Carolina horse nettle (*Solanum carolinense*, pictured at right) and white horse nettle (*S. elaeagnifolium*). Horse nettles grow in agricultural areas, pastures, waste ground and disturbed sites; also along roads, fences, trails and railroad grades. They thrive in sunny areas.

GROWTH: Horse nettle is an erect, branching herbaceous plant that is typically about 2 feet tall, although it can grow to 3 feet. Its hairy stems are armed with sharp spines that can stick in the skin and break off, making it despised by gardeners. Carolina horse nettle flowers are white or pale lavender; white horse nettle flowers are purple.

LEAVES: Alternate, covered with fine, starry hairs on both surfaces. Leaves are irregularly lobed and shaped like a rounded oak leaf; they are up to 7 inches long and are attached to the stem by short petioles (stemlets). The midrib undersides and parts of the veins have small but sharp thorns. Leaves of white horse nettle have a silvery cast, giving it the alternate common name of silverleaf nightshade.

FRUIT: A round, many-seeded berry, up to 1 inch in diameter at maturity. Fruits are borne in drooping clusters on a leafless, thorny stem. Immature berries are bright green with darker, somewhat blotchy stripes. Green fruit is toxic, and is sometimes blamed for cattle deaths. When ripe, the glossy yellow-to-orangish berries resemble small, yellow tomatoes. Ripe berries smell foul and are reported to be toxic in large quantities.

SEASON: Flowers appear in late spring, and bloom all summer. Fruits develop a week or two later, and can be found through early fall.

COMPARE: Horse nettle resembles eastern black nightshade (pg. 248), which has similar flowers, fruits and leaf shape. However, nightshade has no spines; its fruits are much smaller, and are black when mature.

NOTES: Despite its common name, horse nettle is a member of the nightshade family, not the nettle family (*Urtica* spp.). It is resistant to herbicides and is considered a noxious agricultural pest.

green = key identification feature   *combined range

Ripe fruit

TENDER
VINE

OPPOSITE
LEAVES (TYP.)

SUMMER

* see below

Air Potato –OR– **Chinese Yam** *Dioscorea oppositifolia*

HABITAT: This non-native vine is found in moist areas, including thickets and ravines, alongside streams and drainage ditches, on waste ground and along fencelines, and in rich floodplain forests. It grows in shade or sun.

GROWTH: A twining, non-woody vine that grows to 15 feet long, air potato climbs over trees and shrubs, smothering them with its dense foliage. Its slender, round stems wind from left to right around supporting plants.

LEAVES: Leaves are heart-shaped and smooth, with smooth edges; the leaves taper to a point at the tip. The base is often deeply notched and flanked by a pair of rounded lobes. Leaves typically grow oppositely on long petioles (stemlets), although they may grow alternately at the upper reaches of the vine. Each leaf has a central vein and three or four pairs of side veins that curve to follow the edge; all veins originate from the same point at the base. Leaves are typically up to 4 inches long and one-half as wide at the base; they are bright green, although leaf edges, petioles and new growth may be reddish or bronze. Leaves turn yellow in fall.

FRUIT: Aerial tubers (bulbils) that resemble tiny, warty, tan potatoes grow from leaf axils; they are up to 1½ inches across, but often smaller. Some reports say the bulbils are edible but do not detail preparation; it's best to consider them inedible. The underground tuber is edible when cooked.

SEASON: Whitish flowers with a spicy fragrance appear in summer, giving the plant its other common name, cinnamon vine. Aerial tubers develop at the leaf axils from mid through late summer; they drop off in fall.

COMPARE: Leaves resemble some *Smilax* species (pg. 252), but *Smilax* species produce clusters of dark berries. Two native yam vines, four-leaf yam (*D. quaternata*) and wild yam (*D. villosa*), grow in our area; they are much less aggressive in their growth and do not produce aerial tubers.

NOTES: Air potato was planted in the southeast as an ornamental vine. It was first observed as an escapee from cultivation in the late 1980s; since then, it has spread rapidly and become a noxious, invasive pest. Some sources list this plant as *D. batatas* or *D. polystachya*.

green = key identification feature   *specific IN locations not available

TREE

ALTERNATE
LEAVES

LATE SUMMER
TO EARLY FALL

Callery Pear

Pyrus calleryana

HABITAT: Callery pear is a non-native plant that has been widely planted as an ornamental; it is increasingly found in the wild, where it is considered a pest tree in some areas. It is tolerant of a wide variety of habitats, and is found in urban woodlots, abandoned fields, industrial parklands and disturbed areas, where its seeds were likely deposited by birds.

GROWTH: A medium tree, up to 40 feet in height, with a straight trunk and a pyramid-shaped crown. The trunk has furrowed gray or gray-brown bark. Branches are reddish-brown to gray; most are smooth, with gray lenticels (breathing pores). Branches are often armed with thorns.

LEAVES: Glossy, thick, leathery leaves, up to 3 inches long and two-thirds as wide, grow alternately or in clusters on long pale petioles (stemlets). Leaves have pointed tips and are broadest near the base; they often fold in slightly along the midline. Edges are finely serrated, and may appear wavy. Leaves turn scarlet, yellow or purple in fall.

FRUIT: A round, bronze-colored pome with tiny, light speckles and rough skin; the fruit is generally about ½ inch across. Callery pears grow on a thick, orangish stemlet and have a small crown on the bottom. They often grow with the crown end up, looking like a speckled bronze crabapple. Callery pears are edible but too small and hard to eat out-of-hand; they can be juiced, puréed or stewed.

SEASON: Callery pears produce strongly scented white flowers in spring; the fruits follow, and are ripe in late summer to early fall.

COMPARE: Crabapples (pg. 170) are similar in growth form, but the fruits are not speckled; crabapple leaves tend to taper at both ends, and are much thinner and rougher than Callery pear leaves. Common pears (pg. 52) have larger fruits that are greenish or yellowish in color, with brown blotches or fine dots.

NOTES: When picked before a frost, the flesh of Callery pears is hard, but it softens when cooked. They are not as tasty as common pears. Callery pears are often referred to as Bradford pears.

green = key identification feature

TREE   ALTERNATE LEAVES   LATE SUMMER TO EARLY FALL

Russian Olive –OR– **Oleaster**   *Elaeagnus angustifolia*

HABITAT: An introduced plant, Russian olive is found in floodplain forests, irrigation ditches and grasslands. It also grows along railroad grades, roads and fencelines. It tolerates seasonal flooding, but also survives in areas that suffer occasional drought. Prefers sun, but will grow in dappled shade. A very adaptable plant.

GROWTH: A small tree, sometimes appearing as a large shrub; up to 20 feet tall, often with a rounded, spreading crown. Branches are silvery when young, maturing to reddish brown; some have small thorns.

LEAVES: Lance-shaped leaves are grayish-green above; the undersides are whitish. They grow alternately and are generally 2 to 4 inches long and one-quarter as wide, with smooth margins and a well-defined midrib. Leaves are rough-textured on both sides.

FRUIT: The oval drupe, about ½ inch long, is yellow when ripe, and is covered with fine silvery scales. Fruits grow abundantly along the stems from short, scaly stemlets. The fruit, although somewhat dry, is usually sweet, and can be eaten raw, pulped to make fruit leather, or cooked for jam. It is quite astringent when underripe; on individual plants, it may remain too astringent to eat even when ripe.

SEASON: Pleasantly scented yellow flowers appear in spring; the fruit follows and ripens in late summer to early fall.

COMPARE: Autumn olive (pg. 154) has a similar silvery appearance, but its leaves are wider, roughly one-half as wide as they are long. Fruits of autumn olive are rounder and smaller, and are red with silvery scales; they are also more sweet and juicy than those of Russian olive. Autumn olive usually has fewer thorns, sometimes no thorns at all.

NOTES: Russian olive was widely planted during the 1800s in disturbed areas; it is good for stabilizing embankments. It also offers cover and food for wildlife. Nonetheless, it is considered invasive in some areas because it shades out native understory plants and spreads rapidly.

green = key identification feature

TENDER
LEAFY PLANT

OPPOSITE
LEAVES

MID TO
LATE SUMMER

* see below

Horse Gentian –OR– Feverwort
Triosteum spp.

HABITAT: Rocky and wooded areas, especially with rich soil; thickets; wooded ridgetops. Prefers areas with dappled sun.

GROWTH: An erect, unbranched, native perennial, 2 to 4 feet in height. Stems are covered with fine, long hairs; leaves are slightly hairy on the edges and the undersides.

LEAVES: Large, oval leaves, up to 8 inches long and one-half as wide, grow oppositely in pairs; the edges are smooth and the leaf terminates in a sharp tip. Leaf pairs grow in intervals along the stem; **each pair is rotated 90° from the previous pair.** Three varieties inhabit our area. Early horse gentian (*Triosteum aurantiacum,* pictured at right) and yellow-flowered horse gentian (*T. angustifolium*) have leaves that are **distinct from one another,** connected to the stem by a tapering neck. Perfoliate horse gentian (*T. perfoliatum*) has **perfoliate leaves, connected at the base** which clasps the stem.

FRUIT: Orange berries, about ⅓ inch in diameter, grow at the leaf axils; typically, three to five berries grow in each axil. Each berry has a **small crown of narrow leaves,** making the grouping of berries appear spiky. The fruit is inedible and will cause intestinal problems if eaten in large quantities, but the seeds of perfoliate horse gentian (sometimes called wild coffee) were roasted and used as a coffee substitute.

SEASON: Reddish-purple flowers (or yellow, in the case of yellow-flowered horse gentian) bloom in early summer, and are followed by elongated green berries, which enlarge and ripen in mid to late summer.

COMPARE: The alternating growth pattern of the leaves, and the flowers clustered in the leaf axils, make horse gentian easy to identify; once the berries develop, this plant can't be confused with any other.

NOTES: Horse gentian attracts bumblebees, which use their long tongues to extract nectar from the long-necked flowers.

green = key identification feature   *combined range

WOODY
VINE

ALTERNATE
LEAVES

LATE SUMMER
TO FALL

American

Oriental

Bittersweet

Celastrus spp.

HABITAT: Found in rich woods, swamp edges, field edges, ravines and disturbed areas. Also grows on bluffs and rocky slopes. Bittersweet grows best and produces more fruit in full sun, but will tolerate light shade.

GROWTH: Two types of bittersweet grow in our area. Both are perennial woody vines, up to 30 feet long, that climb on trees or wrap around shrubs and fences. American bittersweet (*Celastrus scandens*) is native to our area; Oriental bittersweet (*C. orbiculatus*) is an aggressive introduced vine that kills other plants by smothering or girdling them.

LEAVES: The glossy, dark green leaves grow alternately on the vine, which has a slightly twisting habit, sometimes causing the leaves to appear to rotate along the stem; leaves have finely serrated edges. American bittersweet leaves are shaped like an elongated oval, with sharply pointed tips; they are 2 to 4 inches long and about one-half as wide. Leaves of the Oriental variety are rounded in appearance, being nearly as wide as they are long. Leaves of both turn yellow and drop off in fall.

FRUIT: The round berry-like capsule, about ¼ inch across, is green when young, ripening to orangish in late summer. Fruits of American bittersweet grow in clusters at the branch tips; Oriental bittersweet grows in clusters at the leaf axils all along the stem. In fall, the capsules split open to reveal seeds with a shiny, orange-red coating; the insides of the split-open capsule are orange on American bittersweet, yellow on the Oriental variety. The fruits are mildly toxic and should not be eaten.

SEASON: The vine flowers in late spring. Unripe fruits develop in early summer, maturing in late summer and splitting open in fall.

COMPARE: Japanese honeysuckle (pg. 260) is an aggressive, climbing vine with oval leaves, but its ripe fruits are black.

NOTES: The fruits remain on the plants through winter, providing food for ruffed grouse, pheasants, quail, rabbits, songbirds and squirrels. Branches containing clusters of the dried, split-open fruits are used to add color to flower arrangements.

green = key identification feature

Oriental bittersweet

Split capsule of American bittersweet

TREE

ALTERNATE
LEAVES

SUMMER

Peach

Prunus persica

HABITAT: The domestic peach may be found occasionally in the wild in our area. American Indians cultivated peaches in Colonial days, taking seeds with them as they traveled. Wild trees may be survivors of those days, or remnants of gardens planted by farmers or homesteaders; they may also have grown from a picnicker's discarded peach pit. Peaches do best in well-drained, moist soil; they produce more fruit in sunny areas.

GROWTH: A small non-native tree, up to 25 feet tall, with an open, rounded crown. Branches angle strongly upward, giving the plant a distinctive profile. Bark is gray and smooth, with prominent lenticels (breathing pores), becoming reddish, scaly and irregular as it matures; younger branches are smooth and reddish to greenish, with scattered pale lenticels.

LEAVES: A **distinctly narrow** leaf, 3 to 6 inches long and one-third to one-quarter as wide; leaves often **curve backwards, folding along the midrib.** Edges are finely toothed; the top is shiny and dull green, the underside paler. Leaves grow alternately or in clusters on short petioles (stemlets).

FRUIT: An oblong to round drupe, generally 1 to 2 inches across, with a noticeable **vertical cleft**; the large stone is pitted. Ripe fruits are soft and juicy; the skin is **fuzzy**, and **yellow with a reddish blush**, although wild peaches may be lighter in color than domestic peaches. Flavor varies from tree to tree; some are very sweet, while others are tart or slightly bitter. All are edible; there are no toxic look-alikes. Peach leaves, twigs and seeds contain toxins, and should not be eaten.

SEASON: Peaches flower in early spring; fruits are ripe in midsummer.

COMPARE: American wild plums (pg. 174) have similar but shorter leaves; their fruits are reddish-orange with a dusty bloom, but are smooth-skinned rather than fuzzy.

NOTES: When sweet wild peaches are found, they are excellent eaten out-of-hand. Tart or slightly bitter peaches work well for pickling.

green = key identification feature

TREE

ALTERNATE
COMPOUND
LEAVES

LATE SUMMER
THROUGH FALL

* see below

Mountain Ash

Sorbus spp.

HABITAT: Two varieties of mountain ash inhabit our area: the native showy mountain ash (*Sorbus decora*), and the introduced European mountain ash (*S. aucuparia*). They are found on rocky ridges, in sun-dappled woods, and at the edges of forests. They require ample moisture and moderate to full sunlight; showy mountain ash is very cold-tolerant.

GROWTH: A small tree, generally no higher than 30 feet, with spreading branches and an open crown. The bark is smooth and brownish with numerous lenticels (breathing pores) when young, turning rough and gray with age.

LEAVES: Compound leaves with 11 to 17 leaflets grow alternately on the stems; leaflets are narrow with serrated edges, and paler below than above. Leaflets of showy mountain ash are about **2 inches long, with pointed tips**; the overall leaf is up to 10 inches long. European mountain ash leaflets are 1 to 1½ **inches long and coarsely serrated with blunt tips**; overall leaf is 5 to 8 inches long.

FRUIT: Small pomes, each about ⅜ inch across, grow in dense, flat-topped clusters. Fruits are greenish-white when immature; European mountain ash ripens to bright orange, while showy mountain ash ripens to **deep reddish-orange**. It can be difficult to distinguish between species when confronted with them in the field; fortunately, fruits from both are edible. The fruit is somewhat astringent, becoming a bit milder after a frost. It is often used to make jelly, or as a seasoning for meat.

SEASON: Fruits ripen in late summer through fall, and remain on the trees through winter.

COMPARE: The native American mountain ash (*S. americana*) prefers colder climates, and is found in surrounding states but not our area; its leaves are similar to those of showy mountain ash but slightly narrower with a pointed base, and its fruits are bright orange.

NOTES: Mountain ash is an important fall and winter food source for birds including grouse, waxwings and grosbeaks, as well as for black bears.

green = key identification feature

*combined range

EDIBLE

See companion *Cooking with Wild Berries & Fruits of IN, KY and OH* – pg. 96-97

European mountain ash

TREE

ALTERNATE
LEAVES

LATE FALL

Persimmon

Diospyros virginiana

HABITAT: Moist, well-drained areas including river bottoms, edges of streams, mixed-wood and hardwood forests. Persimmon tolerates damp soil and shade, but it produces more fruit in sunny areas.

GROWTH: This native tree can reach heights of 50 feet, although it is usually much shorter. Bark of a mature tree is dark gray, with raised, blocky patches, similar to flowering dogwood (pg. 178); the trunk often appears orangish between the raised areas. Twigs are light reddish-brown and hairy; they develop a zigzag habit as they mature.

LEAVES: Leaves are roughly oval, up to 6 inches long and one-half as wide, broadest below the midpoint, with a softly pointed tip. They are deep green and smooth on top, paler underneath. They grow alternately on ½- to 1-inch-long downy petioles (stemlets). Edges are untoothed; the midvein is prominent, especially on the underside, and the leaves are slightly folded along the midvein.

FRUIT: A globe-shaped berry, generally 1 to 1½ inches across; the sepals (outer petals) remain on the fruit, forming a sturdy crown (like a thick strawberry cap), and there is a slender flower remnant on the base. The fruit has a whitish bloom; it has up to eight flat, brown seeds, and a jam-like, sticky interior when ripe. When unripe, the fruit is extremely astringent, but when it ripens to deep orange and becomes soft and wrinkly, it is sweet and delicious. There are no toxic look-alikes.

SEASON: Flowers bloom in late spring; the fruit is green and hard most of the summer, ripening to deep orange in late fall, well after the leaves drop. It may remain on the trees through much of the winter. Some foragers wait to pick persimmons until they can be shaken from the tree or drop on their own, an indication of ripeness (Mike Krebill).

COMPARE: Persimmon leaves resemble those of blackgum (pg. 240), but blackgum produces small, oval drupes that are bluish when ripe.

NOTES: Persimmon wood is very dense, and is a favorite of woodworkers; it is also used to make pool cues and the heads of golf clubs.

green = key identification feature

Bark

Ripe fruit

Green fruit

TENDER
LEAFY PLANT

SINGLE
COMPOUND
LEAF

LATE SPRING
THROUGH
SUMMER

* see below

Strawberries

Fragaria spp.

HABITAT: Prefers well-drained soil in full sun to part shade. Often found in rocky areas alongside rural roads, streams and lakes, and in open woodlands, disturbed areas, meadows and fields.

GROWTH: Two types of native wild strawberries inhabit our region: the Virginia or wild strawberry (*Fragaria virginiana*), and the less-common woodland strawberry (*F. vesca,* listed as endangered in Indiana). Both are erect, leafy plants 4 to 8 inches high, with white, 5-petaled flowers. Since both types spread by runners (horizontal stems), it's not uncommon to find a good-sized patch of wild strawberries.

LEAVES: The coarsely toothed, three-part leaf grows at the end of a long, fuzzy stem. The terminal tooth of a woodland strawberry leaf is longer than the surrounding teeth, while it is shorter than the surrounding teeth on a Virginia strawberry, helping distinguish the two varieties.

FRUIT: The heart-shaped strawberry is technically not a fruit; the actual fruits are the darker seeds embedded on the surface of the swollen receptacle (the base of the flower, which is normally inside the fruit). Woodland strawberries are about ½ inch long when mature; the seeds sit on the surface of the receptacle. Virginia strawberries are slightly smaller, and the seeds are slightly embedded in depressions on the surface of the receptacle. Both are rich red when ripe. Strawberries continue to flower throughout summer, so flowers and fruit are present at the same time once the season gets going.

SEASON: Strawberries flower from late spring through midsummer; tiny yellow fruits follow the flowers, swelling and ripening to a juicy red fruit a week or two later. Strawberries often produce fruit all summer.

COMPARE: Mock strawberries (pg. 90) have globe-shaped fruits with red seeds on the surface. The dwarf red raspberry (pg. 124) has similar trifoliate leaves and red fruit, but the fruit is a compound drupe.

NOTES: Although smaller than commercial varieties, wild strawberries are sweeter and more intensely flavored, and well worth seeking.

green = key identification feature

*combined range

Virginia strawberry

Woodland strawberry

TENDER
LEAFY PLANT

COMPOUND
LEAVES

SUMMER

Red Baneberry

Actaea rubra

HABITAT: This native plant grows in shady areas of moist hardwoods and mixed-wood forests. Often found in dappled woods alongside bracken fern and large-leaved aster.

GROWTH: Two to four doubly compound leaves, each up to 15 inches long, grow alternately on the main stem. The total height is 1 to 2½ feet. Flowers grow on a separate, leafless stalk that branches off one of the leaf stalks and generally rise above the surrounding leaves.

LEAVES: Three large compound leaflets grow on each of the long leaf stalks attached to the main stem; each has three or five smooth, sharply toothed leaflets oppositely attached by short stalks. The terminal leaflet is often slightly larger than side leaflets.

FRUIT: Firm, glossy berries about ⅜ inch long, slightly oval to round with a shallow vertical groove. Each berry has a small black dot at the bottom. Berries are typically red, although sometimes they are white. Berries grow in a cluster at the top of the thin flower stalk, and are attached to the stalk by thin, green stemlets. The berries are toxic.

SEASON: Ripe berries can be seen from early through late summer.

COMPARE: The related white baneberry (pg. 304) has similar leaves, but the flower stalk and stemlets are thick and knobby, usually reddish-pink, while those of the red baneberry are green and thin; the dot on the bottom of the berry is larger on white baneberries. Berry color is not always an accurate indicator of species, since red baneberry sometimes has white berries; the appearance of the flower stalk is a reliable indicator.

NOTES: All parts of the plant should be considered toxic; contact with leaves may cause skin irritation in sensitive individuals. Ingestion of the berries may lead to dizziness, vomiting or cardiac arrest; children are especially susceptible. Birds eat the berries with no ill effect, helping disperse the seeds.

green = key identification feature

Red baneberry
with white berries

TENDER
LEAFY PLANT

ALTERNATE
LEAVES

SUMMER

Goldenseal

Hydrastis canadensis

HABITAT: This native plant is found in moist, shady deciduous woods, slopes, ravines and forest edges. Goldenseal prefers loamy soil that is rich with organic matter; it often is found in seasonally flooded areas.

GROWTH: A fuzzy stem grows from the yellowish rhizome (an underground root-bearing stem) to a height of 6 to 18 inches; a large palmately lobed leaf grows at the top of the stem. Some plants have a forked stem, with a leaf on top of each fork; only forked plants will flower and produce fruit. Goldenseal usually grows in large colonies.

LEAVES: The flowering/fruiting plant has two palmately lobed leaves. One leaf is usually larger, up to 9 inches long and nearly as wide; a smaller leaf bears the fruit atop a short stemlet. Each leaf has three to seven lobes with toothy edges. Leaves are hairy on both surfaces, and are sometimes very wrinkly.

FRUIT: Ripe goldenseal fruit is a red, compound drupe about ½ inch across that somewhat resembles a red raspberry (pg. 124). Individual drupes of goldenseal are somewhat pointed, whereas the drupes of raspberries are rounded and more closely joined. The fruits are mildly toxic and should not be eaten.

SEASON: Fruit is green in late spring, ripening to red in midsummer.

COMPARE: Mayapple (pg. 60) has a similar growth habit, with a forked stem topped by a large leaf; however, the fruits bear no resemblance to one another. Red raspberries (pg. 124) somewhat resemble goldenseal fruit, but raspberries have compound leaves.

NOTES: Goldenseal (particularly the rhizome) contains the alkaloids berberine, hydrastine and canadine, and has been used medicinally since pre-Colonial times. It has been used to treat everything from cancer, poor appetite and diarrhea to fever, stomach problems, ringworm and earache. It has recently come into use as an augment for the immune system. Overharvesting and habitat loss have endangered native stocks of the plant, and it is now listed as an endangered species.

green = key identification feature

TENDER
LEAFY PLANT

WHORLED
LEAVES

SUMMER

* see below

Trillium

Trillium spp.

HABITAT: Five species of native trillium with reddish to purplish-red fruits inhabit our area. Two, toadshade (*Trillium sessile*) and bent trillium (*T. flexipes*), are relatively widespread. Red or purple trillium (*T. erectum*) and painted trillium (*T. undulatum*) are found in parts of northeastern Ohio and eastern Kentucky. Sweet Betsy (*T. cuneatum*) is found in extreme southern Kentucky. All inhabit rich, shady forests with ample moisture.

GROWTH: A single stem, 4 to 12 inches in height, has a whorl of three broad, oval leaves at the top. The flower grows from the center of the leaf whorl. After blooming, the sepals (leaf-like structures at the base of the flower) dry out but remain on the plant during fruit development.

LEAVES: Most trilliums listed here have leaves that are solid green, 2 to 7 inches long and nearly as wide; all have smooth edges and pointed tips. Two have mottled leaves; toadshade's are less than 4 inches long with small amounts of white mottling, while sweet Betsy's are up to 7 inches long and heavily mottled with silver.

FRUIT: Trillium have berry-like capsules with three internal chambers containing seeds surrounded by wet pulp; fruits of all but one of the species listed here are reddish to purplish-red with six sharply defined ridges. Fruits of bent, red and painted trillium sit above the leaves on a long stalk rising from the center of the leaf whorl. Bent trillium fruit is ¾ to 1½ inches long. Red trillium fruits are about ¾ inch long; toadshade and sweet Betsy fruits are the same size but have no stalk, sitting directly on top of the leaves. Painted trillium fruits are scarlet and lack defined ridges; they are up to ¾ inch long and egg-shaped.

SEASON: Trillium flowers in the spring; fruits ripen in midsummer.

COMPARE: Four trillium species in our area have similar growth habits, but ripe fruits are greenish.

NOTES: Some trillium fruits are edible, while others are considered toxic. However, the plants are listed as endangered in many locations and fruits should not be disturbed.

green = key identification feature   *combined range

Red trillium fruit

Toadshade trillium flower

Ripe toadshade trillium fruit

TENDER
LEAFY PLANT

ALTERNATE
COMPOUND
LEAVES

MID TO
LATE SUMMER

Mock Strawberry
–OR– Indian Strawberry

Duchesnea indica

HABITAT: Originally from Asia, mock strawberry is sometimes planted as an ornamental, and has escaped cultivation to become a pest in many areas. It is found in parks, lawns, open woodlands, fields and waste ground, growing best in partial shade.

GROWTH: A low-growing plant that creeps along in vine-like fashion. The trailing stem is hairy, and green to purplish-green; it roots at leaf nodes, often forming large, mat-like colonies. Individual stems may be a foot or more in length.

LEAVES: Three-part compound leaves grow alternately on long, hairy green petioles (stemlets). The oval leaflets have rounded teeth around the entire edge; they are up to 2½ inches long and two-thirds as wide. Leaves have fine hairs on the top surface; underneath, the veins are also hairy.

FRUIT: A soft, fleshy red globe whose surface is covered with raised red seeds, the mock strawberry looks like a round, red-seeded version of the familiar strawberry. Mock strawberry grows upright on a hairy stem that arises from the leaf axils; green bracts (leaf-like structures) grow around the base of the fruit. The interior is pale pinkish-white. Although edible, mock strawberries are almost tasteless, and the faint flavor they do have is mildly unpleasant.

SEASON: Yellow flowers appear in profusion from late spring through mid-summer; fruits are ripe from midsummer through late summer.

COMPARE: True strawberries (pg. 82) look similar, but the seeds on the surface are dark and the plant is not vine-like; leaves are toothed only on the top half, while the lower half of the leaf is smooth-edged. True strawberries have white or pale pink flowers.

NOTES: Some references list this plant as *Potentilla indica*.

green = key identification feature

Typical colony

TENDER
LEAFY PLANT

OPPOSITE/
WHORLED
LEAVES

MID TO
LATE SUMMER

Bunchberry

Cornus canadensis

HABITAT: This native plant inhabits cool, shady coniferous and mixed-wood forests; sometimes found in boggy or swampy areas.

GROWTH: Technically a shrub, bunchberry grows as a leafy plant that is typically 4 to 8 inches high. It grows from a spreading rhizome (an underground root-bearing stem) and is often found in a large colony.

LEAVES: Each plant has one or two groupings of four to six leaves that grow oppositely; pairs grow so closely spaced on the stem that the leaf groups have a whorled appearance. The deep green, shiny leaves are oval, with pointed ends and deep veins that curve from base to tip; they are typically 1 to 3 inches long, and about three-quarters as wide. A flower stalk rises from the center of the top leaf pair.

FRUIT: Round, bright red drupes, ¼ inch across, grow in a cluster from the flower stalk at the top of the plant. The fruits are edible, but mealy and bland with hard seeds, and are not worth seeking out. They can be eaten raw as a trail nibble, or cooked into jam, jelly, sauce or pudding. Bunchberry is a good survival food to know about.

SEASON: Tiny greenish flowers with large white bracts (leaf-like structures) appear from late spring through early summer; the flowers develop into fruits, which ripen in mid to late summer.

COMPARE: Canada mayflower (pg. 104) has leaves that somewhat resemble those of bunchberry, but Canada mayflower has only one to three leaves per plant, and its veins are much less pronounced. (A leaf of Canada mayflower is visible in the photo at right, just above the sliver of white wood to the right of the top bunchberry plant.)

NOTES: Bunchberries have a unique pollination method; when the closed flower is touched, it opens explosively—in less than a millisecond—to release its pollen, throwing it up to an inch away at a speed of 10 feet per second (according to a study reported in a 2005 edition of the journal *Nature*). Bunchberry is classified as endangered in Indiana, and threatened in Ohio.

green = key identification feature

TENDER
LEAFY PLANT

COMPOUND
BASAL
LEAVES

MID TO
LATE SUMMER

Jack-in-the-pulpit

Green dragon

Jack-in-the-Pulpit –AND–
Green Dragon

Arisaema spp.

HABITAT: Both are found in areas with rich, moist, well-drained soil such as rocky woodlands, ravines and at the bases of bluffs. Jack-in-the-pulpit (*Arisaema triphyllum*) is found in areas with dappled sunlight; green dragon (*A. dracontium*) can tolerate partial to fairly deep shade.

GROWTH: Both are native perennials, 1 to 3 feet in height, with one or two thick stalks; each is topped by a compound leaf. The flowering portion grows on a separate, thick stalk arising from the base of the leaf stalks. A tubular green sheath (called a spathe) surrounds the clublike structure (called a spadix) that bears the actual flowers. On Jack-in-the-pulpit, **the spathe extends over the top of the spadix, forming a hood**; on green dragon, the top of the spadix becomes **thin and whip-like, extending several inches beyond the spathe** and resembling a dragon's tongue.

LEAVES: Both have a single compound leaf atop each leaf stalk. Jack's leaves are **three-parted**; leaflets are up to 6 inches long and broadly oval, with a sharply pointed tip. Green dragon's leaves have a **wishbone- or arc-shaped stem** that joins the stalk at its center, often appearing to be two separate leaves that grow opposite one another; each leaf has **seven to 15 unequally sized oval leaflets**. Leaves of both have usually died back or fallen over by the time the fruit is ripe.

FRUIT: On both plants, an **elongated, tightly joined cluster of shiny berries** develops from the spadix; ripe berries are bright red. Individual berries are about ⅜ inch across; the cluster is 1 to 3 inches in height and about one-third as wide. The berries are mildly toxic and should not be eaten.

SEASON: Fruits ripen gradually, turning solid red in mid to late summer.

COMPARE: Red baneberry (pg. 84) has a loose cluster of red fruits, and several doubly compound leaves. American ginseng (pg. 108) has a tight cluster of red fruits with three or more five-part compound leaves.

NOTES: All parts of the plant contain calcium oxalate crystals, which cause an intense burning sensation if eaten.

green = key identification feature

Jack-in-the-pulpit

Ripe fruit

Green dragon

TENDER
LEAFY PLANT

ALTERNATE
LEAVES

MID TO
LATE SUMMER

Asparagus

Asparagus officinalis

HABITAT: This escapee from cultivation is found in sunny pastures, fields, roadsides and ditches, and along fencerows, embankments and railroad grades, especially those near agricultural areas.

GROWTH: Asparagus is a commonly grown vegetable that develops into a bushy, multi-stemmed fern-like plant with **feathery, drooping fronds**. It can grow up to 6 feet in height, with equal width. In midsummer, small berries develop on the fronds.

LEAVES: The true leaves are actually **small scales on the main stem**; they are the same as the dark, dagger-like leaves on the stalk of the familiar asparagus spear. The wispy, fern-like appearance of the plant comes from branches with soft, needle-like leaves; the branches grow alternately on the main stem.

FRUIT: Round red berries, about ¼ inch across or slightly larger, grow on thin, bent stemlets from the upper wispy branches. The berries contain toxins and should not be eaten.

SEASON: Asparagus shoots develop into the "asparagus fern" by early summer. Berries soon develop; they are green at first, ripening to red by mid to late summer.

COMPARE: Asparagus is easy to identify at all stages. At a distance, the fern stage of the plant may resemble any number of overgrown leafy plants, but close inspection of an asparagus plant, with its scale-like leaves on the stalks, will confirm its identity. Check the base of the plant; you'll see the asparagus spears you're familiar with, but the pointy top has grown into the fern-like stems. You may even be able to see last year's withered, browned stalks (see small photo at right). Remember the location, and come back the following spring to harvest fresh, wild-grown asparagus spears.

NOTES: Wild asparagus is simply the cultivated vegetable that has escaped the farm or garden. Birds eat the red berries, and the wild plants are often found near farms that grow asparagus.

green = key identification feature

Closeup of base

Asparagus plant in "fern stage"

TENDER
LEAFY PLANT

OPPOSITE
LEAVES

LATE
SUMMER

Partridge Berry –OR–
Two-Eyed Berry

Mitchella repens

HABITAT: Deciduous and mixed-wood forests with rich, acidic soil; also found in bogs, along streambanks and in areas with sphagnum moss. Often found in the same areas as Indian cucumber (pg. 186). The plant tolerates dry to moist soil.

GROWTH: A creeping, ground-hugging native plant that roots at the leaf nodes, spreading to form a low mat on the forest floor. It is typically 2 inches in height or less.

LEAVES: Rounded, glossy, deep green leaves, broad at the base and tapering to a rounded point, grow opposite one another on the long, trailing stem. Leaves are ½ to ¾ inch long and slightly less wide; they are attached to the stem with short petioles (stemlets). The midrib is thick and lighter in color; undersides are yellowish. Leaf edges are smooth.

FRUIT: The smooth drupe, about ¼ inch across, has two small dimples or depressions, formed when the paired flower buds grow together. This gives rise to the common name "two-eyed berry." The fruit is red when ripe; there are no toxic look-alikes because the two "eyes" are very distinctive. The drupe is edible but not tasty, and is not worth seeking out.

SEASON: Partridge berry produces white to pale pink flowers in early summer; the flowers are followed by the fruit, which ripens in late summer and may persist over winter if not eaten by birds.

COMPARE: Cranberry (pg. 118), creeping wintergreen (pg. 120) and bearberry (*Arctostaphylos uva-ursi*; in our area, found only rarely near the Great Lakes) are small, trailing plants like partridge berry, but leaves on these other plants are alternate, and fruits lack the two dimples. All three are edible, so a mistake in identification would not be serious.

NOTES: In years past, partridge berry sprigs were gathered during the winter holidays for use in decorative "partridge berry bowls"; tea made from the leaves was used by American Indian women to aid in childbirth.

green = key identification feature

Closeup

TENDER
LEAFY PLANT

ALTERNATE
LEAVES

LATE
SUMMER

Common False Solomon's Seal

Maianthemum racemosum

HABITAT: This native plant is common and widespread in deciduous or mixed-wood forests. Also grows in waste ground.

GROWTH: The single stem usually grows in a zigzag fashion, bending slightly at each leaf axil; it may be up to 3 feet in length. When young, the stem is upright, but as the plant matures, it typically reclines until it is almost horizontal.

LEAVES: Bright green, shiny leaves are lance-shaped, with a sharp tip at the end; they are up to 8 inches long and about one-third as wide. Leaves are attached directly to the stem in an alternate arrangement, and feature deep parallel veins curving from base to tip.

FRUIT: Smooth, round berries grow in a long cluster at the end of the stem; each berry is about ⅛ inch across. Unripe berries are greenish with tiny purple blotches; ripe berries are deep red. The berries are bitter and generally regarded as inedible, although ripe berries may have been eaten by American Indians in the past (Sam Thayer).

SEASON: Unripe berries are present from late spring through midsummer; berries turn pinkish with red spots before ripening fully in late summer.

COMPARE: Several plants in our area appear similar, but a closer look distinguishes them. Smooth Solomon's seal (pg. 210) bears fruit at the leaf axils rather than at the end of the stem. Starry false Solomon's seal (pg. 102) has a cluster of fruits at the end of the stem, but the plant is shorter, generally 2 feet or less, and the leaves are narrower. It tends to be more upright rather than reclining, and the fruits are pumpkin-shaped. Large-flowered bellwort (*Uvularia grandiflora*, shown on pg. 16) is also short, about 2 feet tall; its leaves are perfoliate, and each stem bears a single triangular-shaped green fruit.

NOTES: Another common name for this plant is feathery false lily of the valley. Some scientific texts list it as *Smilacina racemosa*.

green = key identification feature

Unripe berries

TENDER
LEAFY PLANT

ALTERNATE
LEAVES

LATE
SUMMER

Starry False Solomon's Seal

Maianthemum stellatum

HABITAT: This native perennial inhabits cool, moist forests; it grows adjacent to streams, and is also found in sandy areas near marshes. Starry false Solomon's seal is often one of the first plants to grow after a forest fire.

GROWTH: A single stem grows from a rhizome (underground root-bearing stem) to a height of 1 to 2 feet. The plant arches somewhat, but is not droopy.

LEAVES: Lance-shaped leaves, up to 6 inches long and one-quarter as wide, grow alternately from the main stem, which typically bends slightly at each leaf axil. Leaves attach directly to the stem, and are stiff and bluish-green, with prominent parallel veins; they are smooth on top and may be slightly hairy underneath.

FRUIT: A short raceme (a cluster of multiple fruits) of berries grows at the end of the stem. Unripe berries are **green with maroon stripes**, and are shaped like a **small, squat pumpkin** about ⁵⁄₁₆ inch across. The berries turn yellowish, then ripen to dark red with pale specks before turning solid red. Ripe berries are edible raw or cooked, but have a laxative effect if eaten raw. They have a bittersweet flavor, and are reportedly high in vitamin C.

SEASON: Star-shaped white flowers, which give the plant its common name, appear from mid spring to early summer. The green berries follow, ripening to red by late summer.

COMPARE: Please see the discussion of similar plants listed in common false Solomon's seal on pg. 100. Starry false Solomon's seal is most likely to be confused with common false Solomon's seal. Common false Solomon's seal is generally a larger plant, with more leaves and a larger number of berries in the terminal cluster; also, its berries are tiny and round, and are greenish speckled with purple when unripe.

NOTES: Starry false Solomon's seal is sometimes listed in references as *Smilacina stellata*. Ruffed grouse eat the ripe berries in autumn.

green = key identification feature

Unripe berries

TENDER
LEAFY PLANT

ALTERNATE
LEAVES

LATE SUMMER
TO EARLY FALL

Canada Mayflower
–OR– False Lily of the Valley *Maianthemum canadense*

HABITAT: This native species is found in mixed-wood, hardwood or coniferous forests; also occasionally found near bogs and swampy areas. It can grow in sun or shade.

GROWTH: An understory plant that is 3 to 7 inches tall. Thin stems grow from shallow rhizomes (underground root-bearing stems), often forming large colonies. Flowers and fruit are borne in clusters at the top of stems bearing two or three leaves. Stems with a single leaf do not flower.

LEAVES: One to three bright green, shiny leaves grow alternately from a single stem. Leaves are heart-shaped, with a deeply grooved midline and parallel veins that curve to meet at the sharply pointed tip. Bases are rounded and appear to clasp the stem. Most leaves appear to have a slight notch where the base joins the stem. Leaves are 1 to 3 inches long, and nearly as wide at the base. Edges are smooth.

FRUIT: Shiny, round berries are ⅛ to ¼ inch wide and grow in a loose cluster on a stalk growing at the top of the main stem. They are cream-colored with red speckles at first, turning a speckled pink and eventually ripening to solid red. The ripe berries are bittersweet in flavor; they reportedly cause diarrhea, and consumption is not advised.

SEASON: In late spring or early summer, a cluster of white flowers grows at the top of stems bearing two or three leaves; the flowers turn into speckled cream-colored berries by midsummer. They soften and ripen to solid red by late summer or early fall; the leaves have often yellowed and withered by the time the berries are ripe.

COMPARE: Bunchberry (pg. 92) has leaves that somewhat resemble those of Canada mayflower, but bunchberry plants have groupings of four to six leaves, with pronounced veins. Please also see the discussion of common false Solomon's seal and similar plants on pg. 100.

NOTES: Ruffed grouse and woodland rodents eat the berries.

green = key identification feature

Unripe fruit

TENDER
LEAFY PLANT

ALTERNATE
LEAVES

LATE SUMMER
TO EARLY FALL

Yellow Mandarin
–OR– Yellow Fairybells

Prosartes lanuginosa

HABITAT: Moist, rich hardwood forests, particularly in ravines and slopes of hilly or mountainous areas. It prefers shady or sun-dappled areas.

GROWTH: This native perennial is 15 to 35 inches in height; it forks several times, often having a Y-shaped profile. The stems bend slightly at each leaf axil in zigzag fashion; they are downy and typically tan or brownish.

LEAVES: Bright green, lance-shaped leaves, 2 to 5 inches long and one-half as wide with a long tip, are attached directly to the stems in an alternate fashion except for the two leaves at the tip of the stem, which are oppositely attached. Leaves are smooth on top and downy underneath, and feature deep parallel veins curving from base to tip; veins on the underside are densely covered with fine hairs, and leaf edges have fine, short hairs.

FRUIT: One or two smooth-skinned, oblong berries, about ½ inch long, grow on thin stalks at the branch tips; they are bright red when ripe. The berries are edible in moderation, but almost tasteless.

SEASON: Yellowish flowers appear in mid spring; fruits develop in late spring to summer, turning red in late summer to early fall.

COMPARE: Spotted mandarin (*P. maculata*; also called *Disporum maculatum*) is a related plant; in our area it grows in a few counties in southern Ohio (where it is listed as threatened) and in eastern Kentucky. Its flowers are white, speckled with purple; fruit is tan and rough-surfaced with three lobes. Both yellow and spotted mandarin resemble common false and starry Solomon's seal; see pg. 100 for information. Rose twisted-stalk (*Streptopus lanceolatus*) is also similar, but its fruits grow along the entire stem; in our area, it grows in a few counties in Kentucky and Ohio.

NOTES: The Cherokee name for this plant means "frogs fight with it," based on a legend that two frogs once duelled using the lance-shaped leaves as weapons (*Myths of the Cherokee* by James Mooney, 1900). Some sources list yellow mandarin as *Disporum lanuginosum*.

green = key identification feature

TENDER
LEAFY PLANT

COMPOUND
LEAVES

LATE SUMMER
TO EARLY FALL

American Ginseng

Panax quinquefolius

HABITAT: Rich, moist hardwood forests and ravines; often found on north-facing slopes. This native plant prefers shade or dappled sunlight.

GROWTH: A smooth green stalk grows from the rhizome (underground root-bearing stem), with a whorl of compound leaves at the top. A separate, long flowering stalk rises from the joining point of the leaves. The total height of the plant is 12 to 18 inches.

LEAVES: Ginseng plants typically have three compound leaves, although there can be as many as five leaves per plant. Each leaf is on a long petiole (stemlet). Leaves are typically five-parted and about 10 inches across; individual leaflets are roughly oval in shape, with a short stalk, pointed tips, toothy edges and a pronounced midvein. The length of individual leaflets ranges from 3 to 8 inches; frequently, the two leaflets closest to the center of the plant are much smaller than the others.

FRUIT: A tight cluster of shiny red berries grows on a long stalk from the center of the plant; berries are a flattened oval. The berries are inedible.

SEASON: Ginseng flowers in early to mid summer. Berries ripen in late summer to early fall.

COMPARE: The leaves of ginseng resemble those of Virginia creeper (pg. 214), but Virginia creeper is a vine, its berries are blue, and its leaf edges are more coarsely toothed. Sarsaparilla (pg. 242) has a cluster of compound leaves, but the fruiting stalk grows separately from the leaf stalk and is topped with black berries. The bright red berry cluster of ginseng may be mistaken for that of Jack-in-the-pulpit (pg. 94), but Jack has two compound leaves that are three-parted, the stems are thick and purplish, and the red fruit is an oblong cluster 1 to 3 inches tall on a thick stalk that grows from the juncture of the leaf stalks.

NOTES: Ginseng is highly valued for its rhizome, which has medicinal properties. Overharvesting of the wild plants has severely depleted native stocks; now, most ginseng is grown commercially and the wild plant is considered endangered in most of its range.

green = key identification feature

CACTUS

LATE SUMMER
THROUGH FALL

Prickly Pear Cactus

Opuntia humifusa

HABITAT: Prickly pear or devil's tongue is a native cactus that is found in dry, sandy or rocky areas with ample sunlight; it also grows in open pine forests, on prairies, and in scrubby areas. It can tolerate drought.

GROWTH: Prickly pear have **flat, thick pads** that are roughly paddle-shaped; they may stand upright, or may sprawl on the ground. Typically, pads are armed with very sharp **thorns**, some of which grow in **clusters**. Thorn size and quantity varies somewhat from plant to plant, and some individual plants may have few or no thorns. A many-petaled yellow flower grows from a fleshy green fruit that sits on top of the pad. Eventually, the flower falls off, and the fruit ripens to red or maroon.

LEAVES: Prickly pear have no true leaves; the thick pads grow singly or in clusters. They are generally 2 to 4 inches long and one-half as wide.

FRUIT: Shaped like an **elongated cup** or a flat-topped egg, prickly pear fruit (called *tuna*) grows **from the top edge of the pad**, often in rows or clusters. A pale, cupped depression at the top shows where the flower was attached. Fruits are green when young, maturing to red or maroon; ripe fruits usually have a whitish bloom. Fruit size varies from plant to plant; they may be an inch long, or larger than a hen's egg. When ripe, the flesh is bright red, juicy and sweet, with many small, hard seeds. All prickly pear fruits are edible; there are no toxic look-alikes. *Caution: The fruits have fine, sharp bristles; handle with gloves, and singe over a flame before peeling.*

SEASON: Prickly pear generally flower in late spring through summer; fruits ripen in late summer through fall and may persist through winter.

COMPARE: There are more than 50 varieties of prickly pear cactus; most grow in arid areas of the West. Flower color, pad size and fruit size vary between species, but they are all recognizable as prickly pears. When prickly pear are fruiting, they can't be confused with any other plant.

NOTES: The pads are edible when cooked, and have long been a staple food for American Indians; they are also used in Mexican cooking.

green = key identification feature

Flower on top of fruit

WOODY
VINE

ALTERNATE
LEAVES

SUMMER
THROUGH FALL

Climbing Nightshade

Solanum dulcamara

HABITAT: Moist hardwood forests and thickets, swampy areas, waste ground, roadsides and streambanks. Climbing nightshade prefers partial shade and abundant moisture.

GROWTH: A sprawling, non-native vine that produces many slim, scraggly branches that climb over other plants. It can appear as a short plant, but often grows to 10 feet in length, occasionally even longer. Branches are green or purplish and often hairy when young, turning brownish-green, smooth and woody as they mature; the base of the plant is woody. Flowers are bright purple with yellow centers. All parts of the plant have an unpleasant scent when crushed.

LEAVES: Bright green, shiny, heart-shaped leaves grow alternately on the branches; many leaves have two ear-like lobes at the base. The petioles (stemlets) are slightly flattened. Overall leaf length is up to 3 inches; the ear-like lobes span a width of up to 2 inches.

FRUIT: The glossy, many-seeded berry is up to ½ inch long and usually slightly narrower, although it can also be round rather than egg-shaped. Berries are green when immature, turning orange and finally bright red when ripe. All parts of the plant, including the berries, are highly toxic.

SEASON: Berries are produced throughout summer and into fall, remaining on the plant even after the leaves have fallen off.

COMPARE: Eastern black nightshade (pg. 248) has similar fruits, but it has tiny white flowers and its berries are black when ripe; leaves lack the lobes at the base, and the plant is a tender perennial that is only 1 to 3 feet in height.

NOTES: This plant is also called woody nightshade or bittersweet nightshade, a reference to the bittersweet compound dulcamarine which is found in all parts of the plant, but especially the roots. It also contains solanine, a toxic alkaloid found in the green parts of the common Irish potato (*S. tuberosum*) and other members of the nightshade family.

green = key identification feature

WOODY
VINE

OPPOSITE
LEAVES

LATE SUMMER
THROUGH FALL

* see below

Vining Honeysuckles

Lonicera spp.

HABITAT: Four varieties of native vining honeysuckle may be found in our region: grape (*Lonicera reticulata,* pictured at right), limber or twining (*L. dioica*), trumpet (*L. sempervirens,* which some sources consider a garden escapee) and yellow (*L. flava*). They are found in open forests and thickets, rocky areas, clearings, and along streams and ravines.

GROWTH: A climbing woody vine, 10 to 15 feet in length; it may bend down upon itself and appear shrublike. Stems of grape and yellow honeysuckle are finely grooved; trumpet and limber honeysuckle stems become shreddy with age. Trunks of all four have shreddy bark. Yellow, orange or red flowers grow in a cluster at the end of the vine.

LEAVES: Opposite, 1½ to 4 inches long, attached directly to the stem or by a short petiole (stemlet). Grape honeysuckle leaves are widest, and may be almost round; the others are more oval. One or two pairs of leaves at the end of the stem are joined at the bases to form a cup. The cup of grape honeysuckle has a white bloom above; leaves may be slightly hairy below. Limber and yellow honeysuckle cups may have a slight bloom above. Leaf undersides are waxy, whitish and occasionally hairy on limber honeysuckle; undersides are smooth and pale but not bloomy on yellow honeysuckle. Trumpet honeysuckle leaves, including the cup, are semi-glossy and smooth with no bloom.

FRUIT: Smooth, oval berries, ¼ to ⅜ inch long, grow on a stalk in a cluster from the center of the terminal leaf cup; berries have a bump on the bottom, and are reddish when ripe. They are very bitter and inedible.

SEASON: Flowers are present from late spring through midsummer. The berries ripen from late summer through early fall.

COMPARE: Japanese honeysuckle (pg. 260) is a non-native vine that is considered highly invasive; its black berries grow on stubby stalks from the leaf axils, and it lacks the joined leaf cup at the end of the stem.

NOTES: Grape and limber honeysuckle are listed as endangered in Kentucky. Yellow honeysuckle is not found in Indiana or Ohio.

green = key identification feature   *combined range

WOODY VINE

ALTERNATE LEAVES

FALL

Carolina Coralbead
–OR– **Snailseed**

Cocculus carolinus

HABITAT: This native vine is found in areas with moderately rich, moist soil including thickets, bottomlands, streambanks, forest edges, roadsides and open woodlands. It will tolerate partial shade to full sun.

GROWTH: A twining, woody vine that may grow to 12 feet long in our area; it will climb up fences, posts, telephone poles and other plants, or may recline on the ground. Young stems are thin, green and hairy; older stems are woody, with knobby, warty bark on the oldest parts. Coralbead has no tendrils; to climb, it winds itself around the supporting structure. It frequently has dense foliage.

LEAVES: Heart-shaped to triangular leaves, 2 to 4½ inches long and almost as wide, grow alternately on hairy petioles (stemlets) that are up to 4 inches long. Leaves often have three to five rounded lobes; the central lobe is longest, and the overall outline of some leaves is said to resemble an elephant's head. Edges are smooth. Leaves are bright, deep green above, and are smooth or lightly hairy; undersides are paler and downy.

FRUIT: Bright red, glossy drupes, ¼ to ⅓ inch across, grow in hanging clusters from leaf axils; clusters may be up to 6 inches long. Each fruit has a single, flattened seed that is notched on one edge, with a deep dimple in the center; the edge looks like a textured coil, giving the plant its common name of snailseed. The fruits are bitter and inedible.

SEASON: Small, greenish flowers appear in summer; fruits ripen in fall.

COMPARE: The leaves and overall growth form of the plant resemble greenbrier and some other *Smilax* (pg. 252); however, greenbriers have prickles and thorns, which are absent on coralbead. Also, the *Smilax* in our area have fruits that are black when ripe.

NOTES: Coralbead leaves are eaten by deer and cattle; some birds relish the fruits.

green = key identification feature

Leaf resembles an elephant's head

Shell-like seed

VINING
SUBSHRUB

ALTERNATE
LEAVES

LATE SUMMER
TO EARLY FALL

Large cranberry

Small cranberry

Cranberries

Vaccinium spp.

HABITAT: Two species of native cranberry inhabit our region: large cranberry (*Vaccinium macrocarpon*) and small cranberry (*V. oxycoccus*, listed as threatened in Indiana). Both are found in moist, acidic areas such as sphagnum bogs, swampy spots and fens.

GROWTH: A ground-hugging trailing plant; technically a subshrub, but vine-like in growth habit. Stems are slender and **hairless**. Cranberry plants often take root at the leaf nodes, forming dense mats.

LEAVES: Smooth, hairless, leathery evergreen leaves grow alternately on the slender, wiry stems. Leaves of large cranberry are ¼ to ⅝ inch long, **narrowly oval with blunt tips**, and **pale but not white underneath**; edges are flat or very slightly rolled. Leaves of small cranberry are less than ⅜ inch long, **lance-shaped with pointed tips**, and **white underneath**; edges are rolled.

FRUIT: A red egg-shaped berry that is tart, but delicious. Fruits of large cranberry grow on thin stalks **along the stem**; small cranberry fruits grow on stalks **from the tip of the stem**. Large cranberry fruits are about **½ inch across**; small cranberry fruits are ⅜ inch across or less. Both are yellow when underripe, developing a blotchy red blush before ripening fully. There are no toxic look-alikes.

SEASON: Cranberries ripen in late summer to early fall, and may persist on the evergreen plants through winter if not eaten by birds.

COMPARE: Several plants with edible berries have similar appearance. Wintergreen (pg. 120) has larger leaves, up to 2 inches; its fruits are much smaller, and all parts of the plant smell spicy when crushed. Fruits of partridge berry (pg. 98) are much smaller with two small dimples, and the leaves are larger. Bearberry (*Arctostaphylos uva-ursi*; in our area, found only rarely near the Great Lakes) also has smaller fruits; its leaves are up to 1 inch, pointed at the base and broadly rounded at the tip.

NOTES: Cranberries are best when cooked with some sugar, but can be eaten raw. Large cranberry is commonly cultivated in commercial bogs.

green = key identification feature

Large cranberry

VINING
SUBSHRUB

ALTERNATE
LEAVES

FALL

Creeping Wintergreen
–OR– Teaberry

Gaultheria procumbens

HABITAT: These native plants are found in coniferous and mixed-wood forests and clearings, especially in areas with moss and peat. Wintergreen prefers moist conditions and light shade, and will grow in sandy areas as well as sphagnum bogs, rocky windswept heights, and swamp edges.

GROWTH: A ground-hugging, trailing plant, it is technically a subshrub, but vine-like in growth habit. It spreads slowly, and may grow as a small cluster, or as a larger colony. Individual shoots are less than 6 inches in height. All parts of the plant have a minty smell when crushed.

LEAVES: Leathery, shiny, hairless evergreen leaves grow alternately on short petioles (stemlets) or clustered at the tips of the stems. Leaves are oval, broadest at or above the midpoint, with a tapered base and a roundly pointed tip; they are 1 to 2 inches long and two-thirds as wide. Edges have very fine teeth, and the midrib is light in color. Undersides are pale, frequently with scattered black dots. Leaves often turn burgundy-colored in fall.

FRUIT: A glossy, bright red berry, ¼ to ⅓ inch long, with a star-shaped depression on the bottom, hangs below the leaves or dangles above them on a curved stalk. The berry is edible but mealy in texture, with a mild wintergreen taste; it makes a decent trail nibble. There are no toxic look-alikes.

SEASON: Berries ripen in early fall, and will remain on the plant through winter unless eaten by wildlife.

COMPARE: Several small plants with edible red berries also grow in our area; please see the cranberry text on pg. 118 for information.

NOTES: Leaves are often steeped to make a refreshing tea, giving it the common name of teaberry. Upland birds including quail, grouse, wild turkeys and pheasants eat the berries; deer browse on the entire plant.

green = key identification feature

SMALL
WOODY SHRUB

ALTERNATE
LEAVES

SUMMER

Purple-Flowering Raspberry
Rubus odoratus

HABITAT: Forest edges, open woods, clearings, thickets, cliffs and ravines. It produces more fruit in areas with good moisture and moderate sun, but will tolerate light shade and soil that is occasionally dry.

GROWTH: This erect, leafy native shrub is typically 3 to 6 feet in height; it has a suckering habit, and is often found in large clumps or in colonies up to 15 feet wide. New growth and flowering stems are green or reddish and covered with reddish bristles; older stems are greenish to tan and may have bristles but are never thorny. The thickest stems are smooth and brown with peeling bark. Large, fragrant pink flowers that resemble wild roses are present from early summer through midsummer.

LEAVES: Light green leaves that resemble wrinkled maple leaves, 4 to 8 inches long and wide. They grow alternately on long petioles (stemlets), and typically have five pointed lobes, although some may have only three. Edges are coarsely toothy; undersides are paler and may be slightly hairy.

FRUIT: A compound drupe, ½ to ¾ inch across and fairly flat. Fruits are white and hard at first, turning pinkish and finally ripening to rich red. Ripe fruits are very soft and crumbly, with many small seeds; depending on the plant and the growing conditions, fruits may be juicy and delicious, or dry and bland. Ripe fruits detach cleanly from the plant, leaving the receptacle (core) behind; the picked fruit is hollow. There are no toxic look-alikes that are hollow when picked.

SEASON: Fruits appear on the plant in early summer, ripening throughout the summer.

COMPARE: Red raspberries (pg. 124) have similar fruits, but the plants have compound leaves. Thimbleberries (*R. parviflorus*) strongly resemble purple-flowering raspberries, with very similar form, leaves and fruits, but their flowers are white; they do not grow in our area, being found primarily in the western states.

NOTES: Purple-flowering raspberry is listed as threatened in Indiana.

green = key identification feature

SMALL
WOODY SHRUB

ALTERNATE
COMPOUND
LEAVES

SUMMER

American red
raspberry

Dwarf red
raspberry

Red Raspberries

Rubus spp.

HABITAT: Two types of red raspberries are found in our area. American red raspberry (*Rubus idaeus*) grows in open woods and thickets, and along roads and edges. Dwarf red raspberry or red dewberry (*R. pubescens*) prefers moist areas such as low spots in mixed-wood or hardwood forests.

GROWTH: American red raspberries are brambles, sprawling vine-like shrubs that often form a thicket; some found in the wild are native plants, while others are descended from cultivated plants. Stems, called canes, grow to 5 feet in length and are usually arching but may also be upright. Raspberry canes have round, bristly stems but no thorns; young canes are reddish or greenish. Dewberry is a low, vine-like native plant with erect leaves that creeps along the ground and often roots at the tips. Its stems are slightly hairy, with no thorns or bristles.

LEAVES: On both plants, compound, coarsely toothed leaves with sharply pointed tips grow alternately on the stems. American red raspberry leaves are up to 8 inches long; they usually have three to five leaflets, occasionally seven. Dwarf raspberry leaves are 2½ to 4 inches long; all leaves have three leaflets.

FRUIT: The compound drupes of both plants are up to ½ inch across; ripe fruits are soft and red. American red raspberries detach easily from the plant, leaving the receptacle (core) behind so the picked fruit is hollow; dewberries do not separate easily from the receptacle. Both are edible and sweet, although quality and taste varies from one plant to another.

SEASON: Both fruits ripen in midsummer.

COMPARE: Goldenseal (pg. 86) has similar fruits, but its leaves resemble large maple leaves; its fruits are mildly toxic. Underripe black raspberries (pg. 262) and blackberries (pg. 272) resemble American red raspberries, but their canes have large thorns. Dwarf red raspberry leaves resemble those of strawberries (pg. 82) but strawberry fruit is heart-shaped.

NOTES: American red raspberry is one of the first plants to appear in an area that has been cleared or burned.

green = key identification feature

American red raspberry

Dwarf red raspberry

SMALL
WOODY SHRUB

ALTERNATE
COMPOUND
LEAVES

SUMMER

Fragrant Sumac

Rhus aromatica

HABITAT: Well-drained areas including rocky slopes, high streambanks, sand dunes and old pastures. Also found along rural roads and on waste ground. It prefers sun, but will tolerate light shade.

GROWTH: A spreading shrub, 2 to 6 feet tall and up to 10 feet wide. Twigs are smooth and brown, hairy when young but with **no thorns or bristles**; numerous branches usually rise above the mound of base foliage. *Rhus aromatica* is native to our area; however, hybrids are frequently planted in landscaping, and may be seen as non-native escapees in our area.

LEAVES: Glossy three-part leaves with scalloped edges grow alternately on long petioles (stemlets). Leaves are 4 to 6 inches long, dark green on top and lighter underneath. The end leaflet is **joined directly to the two side leaflets** by a long, tapering neck; it is generally larger than the side leaflets. When crushed, the leaves and stems have a **noticeable scent** which ranges, on individual plants, from pleasant to mildly skunky.

FRUIT: Clusters of **rounded, hairy, deep red drupes, each about ¼ inch long**, grow at branch tips. The drupes are lemony-sour, and can be used to make a lemonade-type beverage. There are no toxic look-alikes with hairy, red fruits; however, people who are highly allergic to poison ivy, mangoes, or cashews should avoid all sumacs, which are in the same family and may cause a severe allergic reaction.

SEASON: Fruits ripen in midsummer, and may persist through winter.

COMPARE: Poison ivy (pgs. 42, 306) has three-part leaves that may have scalloped edges, but it has small ribbed berries that are greenish or white; also, the end leaflet of poison ivy has a long stemlet. Skunkbush (*R. trilobata*) is very similar in appearance to fragrant sumac, but its leaves and fruits are slightly smaller and the plant can grow a bit taller; it is a western plant that is not found in our area.

NOTES: Deer occasionally browse on the foliage and twigs; small mammals and birds eat the fruits, particularly in winter. The fruits were reportedly salted and eaten by pioneers.

green = key identification feature

SMALL
WOODY SHRUB

ALTERNATE
LEAVES

MID TO
LATE SUMMER

* see below

Red Currants

Ribes spp.

HABITAT: Three varieties of red currant inhabit our region: the introduced garden red currant (*Ribes rubrum*, pictured at right), the native swamp red currant (*R. triste*) and skunk currant (*R. glandulosum*), also native. All inhabit cool, moist woodlands, swampy areas, clearings and streambanks.

GROWTH: A straggling shrub, generally about 3 feet in height; garden red currant can reach 5 feet in height. Stems are smooth and thornless; older branches are woody. Garden red currant tends to grow in an upright manner, while swamp red currant and skunk currant often sprawl along the ground. Currant shrubs have no thorns.

LEAVES: Attached alternately to the stem by a medium to long petiole (stemlet). Each leaf has three to five distinct lobes, resembling a maple leaf with rounded teeth. Leaves are 2 to 5 inches long; swamp red currant leaves are usually slightly hairy below, while the other two are usually smooth. Leaves of skunk currant have a disagreeable, skunk-like odor when crushed.

FRUIT: Round ¼- to ⅜-inch berries grow in racemes (long clusters of multiple fruits). Immature berries are green, turning red and somewhat translucent when ripe. All red currants listed here are edible; there are no toxic look-alikes. Berries of garden red and swamp red currant are smooth and glossy, and are tart but delicious when used in baking, or cooked into jelly, jam and other dishes. Berries of skunk currant are covered with glands and hairs; some people find them unpalatable.

SEASON: Red currants ripen in mid to late summer.

COMPARE: Black currants (pg. 268) are similar, but the berries are black when ripe. Gooseberries (pgs. 48, 198, 266) have similar leaves and growth habits, but all gooseberries have thorns at the leaf nodes. Gooseberry fruits grow in clusters of two or three, in contrast to currant fruits which grow in a raceme.

NOTES: If you find a currant with red berries, but the berries are hard and opaque, you may have found unripe black currants (pg. 268).

green = key identification feature   *combined range

SMALL
WOODY SHRUB

ALTERNATE
LEAVES

SUMMER
THROUGH FALL

Matrimony Vine –OR– Goji Berry   *Lycium barbarum*

HABITAT: Also called wolfberry, this Asian native is grown as an ornamental and has escaped into the wild. It is found on waste ground and disturbed sites, alongside roads and railroads, and in abandoned agricultural areas. It prefers sun and requires moist, well-drained soil.

GROWTH: A somewhat straggly shrub with weak, thin branches; longer branches droop down, appearing vine-like. The stems are brownish, sometimes mottled with pale gray; thin lengthwise ridges are often present. Older bark is rough. Plants may have short thorns.

LEAVES: Lance-shaped, or sometimes oval with tapered ends. Leaves are up to 2½ inches long and one-third to one-half as wide; the base tapers into a short, wide petiole (stemlet). Leaves grow alternately, sometimes in small clusters. Edges are smooth; the midrib is prominent. Both surfaces are smooth and dull green in color.

FRUIT: Oval berries, ¼ inch long and half as wide, grow on long stemlets from the leaf axils; the berry is joined to the stemlet with a bell-shaped cap. The berries are reddish-orange when ripe, and contain numerous small seeds. Fully ripe berries are edible raw, juiced, cooked or dried. Underripe berries may contain toxins, and should not be consumed.

SEASON: Purple, bell-shaped flowers bloom from late spring through early fall; berries ripen throughout summer and into fall.

COMPARE: Chinese desert thorn (*L. chinense*) is a very similar plant whose leaves are more rounded. Barberry (pg. 138) has similar-appearing fruits, but its leaves are much smaller and the plant is very thorny. Climbing nightshade (pg. 112) is a woody vine with similar berries, but its leaves are much broader and heart-shaped; nightshade berries are toxic.

NOTES: Goji is grown commercially in China; the berries are dried and sold here and abroad for use in cooking. The juice is marketed in the U.S. as a health tonic, often with claims that it will increase longevity, fight cancer and arthritis, cure impotence and boost the immune system. The leaves are used to make tea, and shoots are cooked as a vegetable in Europe.

green = key identification feature

Thorns

SMALL
WOODY SHRUB

OPPOSITE
LEAVES

LATE SUMMER
TO EARLY FALL

American
strawberry-bush

Running
strawberry-bush

Strawberry-bush

Euonymus spp.

HABITAT: American strawberry-bush (*Euonymus americanus*; also called bursting-heart) and running strawberry-bush (*E. obovatus*) are related native shrubs that are found in areas with rich, moist, well-drained soil including thickets, low woods, streambanks, ravines and swamp edges. Both prefer dappled sunlight or shade.

GROWTH: American strawberry-bush is a loose, open shrub that can grow up to 10 feet in height, but is usually much shorter; it produces suckers and often grows as a tangled, chest-high colony. Running strawberry-bush is a ground-hugging, trailing plant, **12 inches in height or less**, that is technically a subshrub but vine-like in growth habit. Young stems of both are smooth and green, becoming purplish or brown with age; they are thin and flexible. Stems of running strawberry-bush often **develop roots where they contact the ground**, creating **large, mat-like colonies**.

LEAVES: Both have opposite leaves that grow on short petioles (stemlets); edges have fine teeth. Leaves of American strawberry-bush are **slender**, 2 to 4 inches long and one-third to one-quarter as wide; they taper on both ends and are broadest at or below the midpoint. Running strawberry-bush leaves are **oval to egg-shaped**, broadest at or above the midpoint with a tapered base and roundly pointed tip; they are up to 2½ inches long and one-half to two-thirds as wide.

FRUIT: Both plants have **warty-looking, rounded capsules**, about ¾ inch across, that grow on thin stemlets from leaf nodes. Capsules are white at first, turning pink or orange and eventually **splitting into sections to reveal two to five seeds with a bright red, fleshy coating**. American strawberry-bush capsules are three- to five-parted; running strawberry-bush are three-parted. Fruits of both are inedible.

SEASON: Fruit capsules are white in midsummer, turning pink or orangish and splitting open to reveal the red seeds in late summer to early fall.

COMPARE: Winged euonymus (pg. 160) is a related tall shrub with fruits that split open to reveal bright red seeds, but the capsules are not warty.

NOTES: Fruits are eaten by wild birds; leaves are browsed by deer.

green = key identification feature

American strawberry-bush

Running strawberry-bush

Ripe fruit

SMALL
WOODY SHRUB

ALTERNATE
COMPOUND
LEAVES

LATE SUMMER
TO EARLY FALL

Rose Hips

Rosa spp.

HABITAT: At least 18 species of roses grow in the wild in our area; some are native, others are introduced. They grow in clearings, thickets and open forests; on waste ground; and along lakes, streams and rivers.

GROWTH: A bushy, multi-stemmed shrub, typically 1 to 4 feet in height, with equal spread; sometimes grows as a bramble (a vine-like shrub with arching branches). Stems are armed with **thorns or prickles**, which may be scattered or may blanket the stem thickly. Bark of larger stems is shiny and typically reddish-brown; smaller stems are green.

LEAVES: Compound leaves, each with three to eleven oval leaflets, grow alternately. Leaflets are bright green above, and typically have fine hairs on the underside; edges are sharply toothed. The compound leaf is typically between 2 to 4 inches long, usually slightly less wide.

FRUIT: The fruits, called hips, develop at the base of the flower; specific characteristics are quite variable. They range in shape from round to oval; ripe hips are typically red, but they are sometimes orange. Hips always have a group of **withered sepals at the end of the fleshy swelling**. All hips are edible, but they are filled with small, hard, bitter seeds and tiny, stiff, irritating hairs. The best hips for eating have a higher flesh-to-seed ratio. There are no toxic look-alikes.

SEASON: Roses bloom from late spring through summer; hips develop afterwards, and are hard and green most of the summer, ripening in late summer to early fall. They typically persist through winter, and become softer and sweeter after a frost.

COMPARE: Roses are easy to identify, especially when hips (or flowers) are present; no other plant compares to a rose.

NOTES: Rose hips are rich in nutrients, particularly vitamin C. They may be eaten raw or cooked; split the hips and scrape out the bitter seeds and irritating hairs before eating. Palatability varies between species and also from plant to plant, so try a few from the plants you've found before collecting too many. Rose hips are often dried and brewed for tea.

SMALL
WOODY SHRUB

ALTERNATE
LEAVES

LATE SUMMER
TO EARLY FALL

Canada Yew

Taxus canadensis

HABITAT: Shady, cool sites in coniferous or mixed-wood forests. Also found along streambanks, edges of bogs and swamps, and other moist, shady areas. Found in old-growth forests, rather than new growth.

GROWTH: A native, **bushy evergreen shrub**, up to 5 feet in height but usually shorter. Branches grow thickly in an upright spray. The bark of larger stems is reddish; older stems may have large, grayish scales. Yew plants are unisexual—a plant is either male or female, and each produces a different type of flower. Only female plants bear fruit.

LEAVES: **Flat, dark green evergreen leaves with sharp tips** grow thickly on soft twigs. The leaves are attached alternately in a spiral pattern; they are **bent at the bases** so they appear to grow in a flat plane from the twig. Leaves are up to 1 inch long, and less than ⅛ inch wide.

FRUIT: A **soft, bright reddish-orange cup** called an aril surrounds a single seed; the aril is about ½ inch wide. Yew arils can be eaten by humans, but the seed and all other parts of the plant are dangerously toxic. It's not worth taking the risk; leave the aril alone, and let the birds eat the seeds (birds won't be harmed by eating them).

SEASON: Fruits are green, hard and small in midsummer, swelling and ripening in late summer through early fall.

COMPARE: A cultivated yew species, Japanese yew (*T. cuspidata*), has the same distinctive fruit and very similar leaves, but it typically grows as a tree; in our area, it is found occasionally in the wild in Ohio and Kentucky.

NOTES: All parts of yew except the aril (seed cup) contain taxanes, highly poisonous alkaloids which are toxic to humans and most animals. Deer, however, are not affected by the alkaloids, and browse extensively on the leaves; in some areas, yew have become scarce due to deer depredation. Birds eat the seeds contained in the aril, but are not harmed because the seeds pass through before the protective seed coat is dissolved. Canada yew is listed as endangered in Indiana and threatened in Kentucky.

green = key identification feature

SMALL
WOODY SHRUB

ALTERNATE
LEAVES

LATE SUMMER
TO EARLY FALL

Japanese Barberry

Berberis thunbergii

HABITAT: This is a cultivated plant that has escaped into the wild; it is drought-tolerant, and highly adaptable. It is often found on the fringes of urban areas, in both moist and dry areas. Also grows in open hardwood or mixed-wood forests, pastures, disturbed areas and meadows.

GROWTH: A dense, rounded shrub with arching branches that often extend beyond the mass of the shrub; 3 to 6 feet in height and slightly wider. Leaf nodes have a thin, sharp thorn, about ½ inch long. The thin, reddish stems are grooved, and zigzag slightly at leaf nodes.

LEAVES: Paddle-shaped, broadest near the tip with a tapering base; deep green, with smooth edges and a deeply cleft midvein. Leaves are ½ to 1 inch long and about one-half as wide, and grow in clusters of two to six; the clusters alternate along the stem.

FRUIT: Oblong, shiny berries grow on a long stalk from the leaf nodes; the berries are usually abundant. Berries are up to ½ inch long, and sometimes so narrow that they appear cylindrical. They are yellowish when immature, ripening to opaque scarlet. The berries are dry, with a sharp, sour flavor; they are dried and used in Mideastern cooking.

SEASON: Berries ripen in late summer to early fall. The red berries often remain on the plant through winter, after the leaves have dropped.

COMPARE: European barberry (*B. vulgaris*) has a similar growth habit, and may be encountered in our region as a garden escapee; however, the berries grow in racemes (long clusters), and its leaf edges are toothy. American barberry (*B. canadensis*) is a native barberry that is very rarely seen in our area and is considered endangered in Kentucky and Indiana; its leaves have five to nine bristle-tipped teeth.

NOTES: Japanese barberry was introduced as an ornamental in the late 1800s; it has escaped cultivation and often crowds out native plants. It also alters soil chemistry by raising the pH level; this often causes native plants to suffer. Birds consume the prolific berries, spreading the plant; it is considered invasive in most areas in which it appears.

green = key identification feature

Thorns and unripe fruit

Ripe fruit

SMALL
WOODY SHRUB

OPPOSITE
LEAVES

FALL

Coralberry –OR– Buckbrush *Symphoricarpos orbiculatus*

HABITAT: This native shrub grows in dry, sunny areas including pastures, abandoned agricultural fields, rocky bluffs, thickets and open woods; often found alongside roads and railroads.

GROWTH: An open, twiggy, multi-stemmed shrub, **up to 4 feet in height** but often shorter; it spreads by rhizomes (underground root-bearing stems) and often forms large colonies. Branches are thin and flexible, often **arching downward**, especially when bearing fruit. Young stems are tan to purplish and downy, later becoming smooth and brown. The trunk has **flaky or shreddy brown bark**.

LEAVES: Egg-shaped, with a rounded or tapered base and roundly pointed tip; 1½ to 2 inches long and two-thirds as wide, broadest at or below the midpoint. Leaves grow oppositely on very short petioles (stemlets); the edges are untoothed, and may have fine hairs (visible with a lens). The top surface is bluish-green and smooth; undersides are paler and typically hairy, with pronounced veins.

FRUIT: Tight, sometimes blocky clusters of round to egg-shaped drupes, each about ¼ inch long, grow at leaf axils and at the tips of the branches; a crown-like floral remnant is present on the base. The fruits are **opaque, rosy reddish-purple** when ripe. They are not edible.

SEASON: Tiny, greenish flowers appear underneath the leaves at the leaf axils in midsummer; fruits develop slowly, ripening in fall. The fruits may persist over winter unless eaten by wildlife.

COMPARE: Bush honeysuckles (pg. 144) have numerous berries along the stem, but they are bright red or orange and translucent. Coralberry also may be mistaken for a young border privet (pg. 284), but privet's leaves are thick and leathery; ripe fruits are black. Bush honeysuckles and privet are much larger than coralberry when mature.

NOTES: The leaves and twigs are browsed by deer and other mammals; birds sometimes nest in the dense growth, and some eat the fruits, although they do not appear to be a favored food.

green = key identification feature

LARGE
WOODY SHRUB

OPPOSITE
COMPOUND
LEAVES

EARLY TO
MID SUMMER

Red Elderberry

Sambucus racemosa

HABITAT: This native shrub is found in our area mostly in the north, where it grows along habitat edges such as roadsides, forest borders, shorelines and fencerows. It also grows in cool woods and in forest openings at higher elevations.

GROWTH: A large, fast-growing native shrub, sometimes appearing as a small tree. Up to 20 feet in height, but also found much shorter. Bark of older stems is gray to reddish-brown, and covered with numerous warty lenticels (breathing pores). Younger stems are soft and pithy, and often covered with downy hairs.

LEAVES: Compound leaves, each with **five to seven leaflets**, grow oppositely on the stem; leaves are 6 to 10 inches long and nearly as wide. Leaflets are 2 to 5 inches long and one-third as wide, oval with a rounded base and pointed tip; edges have fine, sharp teeth. Top sides are dark green and smooth, undersides are paler and may be downy.

FRUIT: Round drupes, about ⅛ inch across, with two seeds, grow profusely in **upright, rounded clusters** atop stalks that rise from the leaf axils; fruits are **bright red** when ripe. The fruits are rank in flavor and somewhat toxic, especially when raw; cooking may render the fruit—but not the seeds—edible, but opinions vary. Leaves, stems and all other parts of all elderberry species are toxic.

SEASON: Berries ripen in early to mid summer, well before those of the common elderberry (see below).

COMPARE: Common elderberry (pg. 200) has similar growth habits, but ripe fruits are purplish-black, and grow in flat-topped clusters rather than the rounded clusters of red elderberry; common elderberry leaves have 5 to 11 leaflets. Fruits of common elderberry are edible when cooked.

NOTES: Red elderberry is one of the first shrubs to flower in the spring. The fruits are eaten by many species of birds. Some sources list this plant as *S. pubens*. Red elderberry is listed as endangered in Kentucky.

green = key identification feature

LARGE
WOODY SHRUB

OPPOSITE
LEAVES

SUMMER
THROUGH FALL

* see below

Bush Honeysuckles

Lonicera spp.

HABITAT: Five types of non-native bush honeysuckle with red or orange-red berries inhabit our region: Amur (*Lonicera maackii*), Tatarian (*L. tatarica*), Morrow's (*L. morrowii*), European fly (*L. xylosteum*) and showy bush honeysuckle (*L. × bella*). All are considered invasive. They inhabit forest edges, parklands and shelterbelts. Highly adaptable, they prefer full sun with ample moisture, but tolerate shade and moderately dry soil.

GROWTH: Multi-stemmed shrubs with spreading crowns. Amur honeysuckle is the largest, **up to 15 feet high with equal spread.** Tatarian honeysuckle is up to 10 feet high and wide; European fly, 8 to 10 feet high and wide; Morrow's and showy bush honeysuckle, up to 8 feet high and wide. Bark on older branches is often shreddy, peeling off in vertical strips.

LEAVES: Opposite, oval leaves, 1 to 2½ inches long, with short petioles (stemlets). Amur leaves are **shiny** and dark green, with a **sharply pointed tip.** Morrow's and showy bush honeysuckle are **blue-green and slightly hairy** underneath; **tips are rounded.** Tatarian honeysuckle's leaves are **blue-green and smooth,** with **a tip that is pointed but not as sharp** as Amur's. European fly's leaves are are **grayish-green and hairy.**

FRUIT: A juicy, round berry, ¼ inch in size; most are red when ripe, but berries of Morrow's and Tatarian are sometimes orange even when ripe. Berries often grow in pairs and may appear to be joined at the base, but **each berry is distinctly round.** Morrow's and Amur honeysuckle berries have a ½-inch stemlet; the berry stemlet is very short on the other three listed here. Fruits of all non-native honeysuckles are bitter and inedible.

SEASON: Bush honeysuckles are one of the first plants to develop leaves in the spring. Ripe berries are present from early summer through fall.

COMPARE: Canada fly honeysuckle (*L. canadensis*), a native shrub found in our area only in northeastern Ohio, does not exceed 5 feet; its red paired fruits are joined at the base and have pointed tips. Also see pg. 162 for information on other shrubs with multiple red fruits along the branches.

NOTES: Birds devour honeysuckle berries, propagating the plants.

green = key identification feature   *combined range; specific locations not available

Amur honeysuckle

Tatarian honeysuckle

Morrow's honeysuckle

LARGE WOODY SHRUB

ALTERNATE COMPOUND LEAVES

MID TO LATE SUMMER

Prickly Ash –OR–
Toothache Tree

Zanthoxylum americanum

HABITAT: Moist, sun-dappled hardwood and mixed-wood forests; woodland borders; river bottoms, ravines and thickets; bluffs and rocky hillsides.

GROWTH: A thorny, multi-stemmed native shrub, typically 8 to 10 feet in height; occasionally up to 25 feet high. Bark is brown or gray; twigs are reddish-brown with white spots. Bark sometimes splits, revealing **yellowish wood**. Stems are armed with **thorns** that are up to ½ inch long. All parts of the plant have a **citrus fragrance**.

LEAVES: Compound leaves, up to 10 inches long, with 5 to 11 leaflets, grow alternately. Leaflets are oval, ¾ to 3 inches long and one-half as wide, with broad bases and softly rounded tips; dull green above, paler below. The terminal leaflet is on a short stemlet; all others attach directly to the greenish stem.

FRUIT: Rounded, berry-like fruits grow in **clusters along the stems**. Fruits are reddish to orangish at maturity, and have a **bumpy texture**. They are technically follicles, dry capsules containing seeds; they split open when ripe to release the shiny black seeds. The fruits are inedible, but in the past they were reportedly chewed to relieve toothache. According to *The Dictionary of Useful Plants* (Nelson Coon; Rodale Press), the seeds may be cooked and used as a pepper substitute.

SEASON: Fruits ripen in mid to late summer, splitting open to release their seeds (one or two per follicle) by summer's end.

COMPARE: There are no confusing look-alikes. Leaves resemble those of the locust family (*Robinia* spp.) but locusts bear fruits that are flat and pod-like. The unusual fruits of prickly ash make this plant unmistakable when it is bearing fruit.

NOTES: The flowers, which are inconspicuous and appear in spring, attract bees. Wildlife, including vireo and other birds, rabbits and chipmunks, eat the fruit; giant swallowtail butterfly larvae eat the leaves.

green = key identification feature

LARGE
WOODY SHRUB

ALTERNATE
LEAVES

LATE
SUMMER

Common Chokecherry

Prunus virginiana

HABITAT: Mixed-wood or hardwood forests, clearings, parklands, thickets, slopes, river and creek embankments. In the northern part of our area, chokecherries thrive in full sun; in the southern part, they require moist areas with partial shade.

GROWTH: A large native shrub, up to 25 feet in height but usually much shorter. Generally open in form and somewhat straggly. Bark is reddish-brown to gray and is smooth, with visible lenticels (breathing pores); smaller stems are often reddish. Shrubs frequently form thickets.

LEAVES: Broadly oval, smooth leaves grow alternately on inch-long petioles (stemlets) that are often reddish. Leaves are dark green above, paler underneath; edges are finely toothed. Leaves are 2 to 4 inches long, roughly one-half as wide, tapering at or above the middle of the leaf to a broad point. The petiole has several small glands (visible with a lens).

FRUIT: Shiny round drupes, ⅜ inch across, grow in racemes (long clusters of multiple fruits). Ripe fruits are bright red, reddish-purple or reddish-black; they are soft and somewhat translucent. Each drupe contains a single egg-shaped pit which is fairly large in proportion to the amount of flesh. Chokecherries have a delicious sweet-tart flavor, although they are quite astringent when eaten raw. There are no toxic look-alikes.

SEASON: Chokecherries ripen in late summer.

COMPARE: Black cherries (pg. 300) have similar long clusters of fruits, but the leaves are much narrower and have reddish hairs along the midrib on the underside. Pin cherries (pg. 172) have narrower leaves; fruits are bright red when ripe and grow in small clusters, each on its own stem, rather than in racemes. Serviceberries (pg. 204) have similar leaves, but the fruit is a pome, an apple-like fruit with a crown on the base.

NOTES: Chokecherry leaves and pits contain hydrocyanic acid, a cyanide-producing compound. The leaves and pits should never be eaten, and care should be taken to avoid crushing chokecherry pits when juicing the fruits. Cooking or drying eliminates the harmful compound.

green = key identification feature

Chokecherry bark

LARGE
WOODY SHRUB

OPPOSITE
LEAVES

LATE SUMMER
TO EARLY FALL

Guelder rose
*see below

Highbush
cranberry

Guelder Rose –AND–
Highbush Cranberry

Viburnum spp.

HABITAT: Moist, sun-dappled mixed-wood forests and thickets; swampy areas; river valleys and streambanks; edges and clearings.

GROWTH: These two similar plants are multi-stemmed shrubs with rounded crowns, up to 15 feet high. Bark is smooth and grayish-brown. Guelder rose (*Viburnum opulus* var. *opulus*), also called European cranberry, is a non-native species that has naturalized in many areas. Highbush cranberry (*V. opulus* var. *americanum;* formerly named *V. trilobum*) is a native plant; it is listed as endangered in Indiana and threatened in Ohio.

LEAVES: Three-lobed leaves with well-defined veins resemble maple leaves; they attach oppositely to the stems on grooved petioles (stemlets). Leaves of guelder rose are typically 2 to 4 inches long and wide; those of highbush cranberry are up to 5 inches long and slightly less wide. Lobes on both are sharply pointed, with numerous irregular teeth on each lobe; highbush cranberry is less toothy. Tiny glands at the base of the leaf stalk, visible with a lens, are concave on the guelder rose, and convex or dome-shaped on highbush cranberry.

FRUIT: Bright, shiny, red drupes grow in large, showy clusters. Individual drupes are ¼ to ½ inch long and slightly narrower. Fruit clusters grow on a long, reddish stalk that grows from the branch tip, beyond the last pair of leaves. Ripe, soft fruits of highbush cranberry are tart but edible, with a taste similar to commercial cranberries; they are used to make jelly, jam or sauce. Guelder rose fruits are very bitter; although edible, they are seldom gathered by foragers. There are no toxic look-alikes.

SEASON: Fruits ripen in late summer to early fall, and may persist on the plant through winter.

COMPARE: Mapleleaf viburnum (pg. 286) is similar, but ripe fruits are black.

NOTES: Highbush cranberries aren't related to true cranberries (*Vaccinium* spp.; pg. 118), but they taste similar, giving them their common name.

green = key identification feature   *specific KY locations not available

Guelder rose

Highbush cranberry

LARGE
WOODY SHRUB

ALTERNATE
LEAVES

LATE SUMMER
TO EARLY FALL

Winterberry

Catberry

Possumhaw

Winterberry, Catberry
–AND– Possumhaw

Ilex spp.

HABITAT: These native shrubs grow in moist locations including damp mixed-wood forests, thickets, pond and stream edges, and swampy or boggy areas. Plants in full sun produce more fruits.

GROWTH: Erect shrubs with many branches; often growing in colonies. Possumhaw (*Ilex decidua*) may be 30 feet in height, although it is usually shorter; winterberry (*I. verticillata*) is 20 feet or less, while catberry (*I. mucronata*) is 5 to 10 feet in height. Bark on mature stems is dark gray to brown, smooth, and mottled with lighter spots. Winterberry and catberry twigs are purplish-brown, while those of possumhaw are light gray; all have scattered lenticels (breathing pores). All are unisexual—a plant is either male or female, and each produces a different type of flower.

LEAVES: Elliptical leaves that taper at both ends are attached alternately to the stems on petioles (stemlets) that are often reddish; leaf undersides are downy. Winterberry's leaves are up to 4 inches long; edges have small, sharp teeth, especially on the top two-thirds. Possumhaw leaves are 2 to 3 inches long with rounded teeth. Catberry leaves are 1 to 2¾ inches long and usually smooth-edged, with a short bristle at the tip.

FRUIT: Smooth, glossy, opaque bright red drupes, ¼ inch across, grow in clusters from the leaf axils of female plants; fruit stemlets are short on winterberry and possumhaw, longer on catberry. The fruits are inedible, and may cause intestinal problems.

SEASON: Fruits ripen from late summer to early fall, and may persist through midwinter, making a striking display.

COMPARE: American holly (pg. 164) has similar fruits, but leaf edges have several long, spine-tipped points. Please also see pg. 162 for information on other shrubs with multiple red fruits along the branches.

NOTES: "Possumhaw" is also used to refer to an unrelated species, *Viburnum nudum* var. *nudum,* which resembles withe-rod (pg. 226).

green = key identification feature

Winterberry

Catberry

Possumhaw

LARGE
WOODY SHRUB

ALTERNATE
LEAVES

LATE SUMMER
TO EARLY FALL

Autumn Olive

Elaeagnus umbellata

HABITAT: Open woodlands, grassy areas, waste ground, roadsides and fencerows. Grows in a variety of soils, from sandy, loamy soil to fairly heavy clay soil with good drainage. The roots fix nitrogen, allowing the plant to thrive in poor soils. Does best in full sun, but tolerates light shade.

GROWTH: A large non-native shrub, up to 15 feet tall with equal width. Somewhat straggly, often considered weedy-looking; tends to form thickets. The entire plant has a **silvery appearance**. Stems are silver-brown, with brown scales. Branches may have scattered small thorns.

LEAVES: **Silvery-green** leaves grow alternately on short, scaly petioles (stemlets). Leaves are elliptic, 2 to 4 inches long and **one-half as wide**, tapering at both ends. Undersides are **silvery and often have brown dots**, especially early in the season. Edges are wavy but untoothed.

FRUIT: Oval to round drupes, ⅓ inch long, are covered with **silver scales**; fruits are plump and red when ripe. Eating quality varies from plant to plant. The best fruits are juicy and delicious; others have an astringent after-taste. Choice fruits can be pulped or juiced; some foragers report that the seeds are edible, with a nutty taste. There are no toxic look-alikes.

SEASON: Fruits are hard, brownish and scaly in early summer; as the season progresses, they turn yellow with brown dots, finally ripening to a juicy red at the end of summer or in early fall.

COMPARE: Russian olive (pg. 70) has a similar silvery appearance, but its leaves are very narrow; ripe fruits are oblong and yellowish. Russet buffaloberry (*Shepherdia canadensis*) has silver scales on the fruit and leaves, but its leaves are opposite; in our area, it is found only rarely in northern Ohio, in the counties bordering Lake Erie. Also see pg. 162 for information on other shrubs with multiple red fruits along the branches.

NOTES: Autumn olive was widely planted during the 1800s in disturbed areas; it is good for stabilizing embankments. It also offers cover and food for wildlife. Nonetheless, it is considered invasive in some areas because it shades out native understory plants and spreads rapidly.

green = key identification feature

Underside of leaf

LARGE
WOODY SHRUB

ALTERNATE
LEAVES

LATE SUMMER
TO EARLY FALL

Northern Spicebush

Lindera benzoin

HABITAT: Rich, moist deciduous woodlands and streambanks. Also found in ravines, valleys and bottomlands. Prefers full sun to partial shade.

GROWTH: A rounded, open native shrub, 8 to 12 feet in height, with equal spread. All parts of the plant have a **spicy scent**, especially when bruised. The bark is dark brown, and has numerous **small, raised, light-colored bumps** scattered along the main stem and older twigs. Spicebush plants are unisexual—a plant is either male or female, and each produces a different type of flower.

LEAVES: Smooth, glossy leaves are oval, tapering on both ends; 2 to 5 inches long, roughly one-half as wide, widest at the midpoint or slightly towards the tip. Edges are smooth; the tip has a sharp point. Leaves are medium green above, lighter below, and grow alternately on the stems on short petioles (stemlets); veins are prominent on both surfaces. Stems often have several leaves, of widely varying sizes, clustered together.

FRUIT: Shiny oval drupes, about ½ inch long, grow on short stemlets in small clusters along the branches of the female plants; fruits are red when ripe. The base has a small indentation. The fruit is used as a seasoning; it has a spicy, fruity flavor similar to allspice. There are no toxic look-alikes that have the spicy scent of spicebush.

SEASON: Fruits are present on the plant starting in midsummer. They are greenish when immature, ripening in late summer to early fall.

COMPARE: Southern spicebush (*L. melissifolia*) is a related species that grows to the south of our area; its fruits are larger and leaves are narrower. It is listed as endangered throughout the U.S. Also see pg. 162 for information on other shrubs with multiple red fruits along the branches.

NOTES: The leaves and twigs can be used to brew a spicy tea. White-tailed deer browse on the plants, as do other woodland mammals including cottontails and opossums. Songbirds, and upland birds such as quail and pheasants, feed on the fruits. The plant is host to the larval stage of the spicebush swallowtail butterfly.

green = key identification feature

LARGE
WOODY SHRUB

OPPOSITE
LEAVES

LATE SUMMER
TO EARLY FALL

Buttonbush

Cephalanthus occidentalis

HABITAT: Swampy and marshy areas; seasonally flooded ground; also along edges of ponds, lakes, rivers and streams. Buttonbush can't survive dry conditions or drought; it does best in full sun.

GROWTH: An open, straggly native shrub, generally 6 to 10 feet in height with equal spread; in favorable conditions, it may be taller. It often grows in dense colonies. Young stems are reddish-brown; older bark is grayish-brown and flaky. The distinctive flowering head is a 1-inch ball with numerous, tiny white flowers with thin, protruding stalk-like styles (the part of the flower that has the pollen-collecting part on its tip); the overall effect is that of a flowery pincushion stuck with many pins.

LEAVES: Glossy, smooth, bright green leaves grow oppositely on thin petioles (stemlets); some also grow in small whorls. Leaves are 3 to 5 inches long and one-third to one-half as wide; they are roughly oval, with a tapered base and a sharply pointed tip. Leaf edges are smooth; the midrib and veins are prominent.

FRUIT: A dull red ball, about ¾ inch across, with **numerous blunt nutlets** that give the ball a **nubby appearance**. The fruiting ball often persists through the winter. The fruits and leaves are toxic.

SEASON: Buttonbush flowers in the middle of the summer; the fruits replace the flowers in late summer, and are green at first, ripening to dull red in late summer to early fall.

COMPARE: When buttonbush has flowers or fruit on it, it is unmistakable and can be confused with no other plant.

NOTES: American Indian peoples in the southern United States used a tonic made from buttonbush bark to treat intestinal problems. Bees and many kinds of moths and butterflies are attracted to buttonbush flowers; waterfowl eat the fruits.

green = key identification feature

NOT EDIBLE

LARGE
WOODY SHRUB

OPPOSITE
LEAVES

LATE SUMMER
TO FALL

Winged Euonymus

Euonymus alatus

HABITAT: This fast-growing Asian native has been widely planted as an ornamental, and has escaped cultivation to become a nuisance in the wild. It is found in moist, well-drained areas including forest edges, shelterbelts, highway embankments, woodlands and old fields.

GROWTH: A multi-branched shrub up to 20 feet in height; it spreads by suckering and is sometimes seen in wide, tangled masses that can be 50 feet or more in width. Young twigs are green, turning gray and bumpy; as the branches mature, they develop two to four flat, wing-like bark extensions along the branches.

LEAVES: Oval leaves, 1 to 3 inches long with a tapered base and a pointed tip grow oppositely on very short petioles (stemlets). Leaf edges are finely toothed; summer leaves are dull green on top, paler underneath. In fall, leaves gradually turn a vivid magenta-pink; it's common to see a leaf that is part green and part pink.

FRUIT: Egg-shaped, dull pink capsules, about ½ inch long, grow on long stemlets from the leaf axils. Mature capsules split open to reveal seeds with a shiny, bright orangish-red coating. The fruits are inedible.

SEASON: Inconspicuous greenish flowers first appear in spring, and may be present through late summer. The pink capsules develop in late summer, splitting open in early fall.

COMPARE: Wahoo or burning bush (*E. atropurpureus*) is a native plant with similar leaves, growth form and fall color; however, the fruits are four-lobed capsules and the stems lack the wing-like extensions. Wahoo grows throughout Indiana and Ohio, and is also found in much of northern Kentucky.

NOTES: When winged euonymus is in its fall color, it is a stunning plant; it's easy to see why it is frequently used as a landscape specimen. Unfortunately, its aggressive growth habits crowd out native plants, and it is considered an invasive pest. Birds eat the seeds, helping to propagate the plant.

green = key identification feature

Winged
bark

LARGE SHRUB
OR SMALL TREE

ALTERNATE
LEAVES

MIDSUMMER
TO FALL

Carolina Buckthorn

Frangula caroliniana

HABITAT: Moist, rocky areas, including bottomlands, ravines, dappled woodlands, streambanks and thickets. It prefers partial shade.

GROWTH: This native plant grows as a large shrub or small tree, up to 20 feet in height but typically shorter. It usually has multiple stems at its base and tends to be fairly open, but in areas of full sun, its growth becomes more dense. Twigs are greenish to reddish, turning gray with age; new growth is downy. The trunk is grayish-brown, often mottled with light patches; bark of old trunks often has vertical fissures.

LEAVES: The long oval leaves are almost lance-like; the bases are slightly rounded and the tip is softly pointed. Leaves grow alternately on pale ½-inch petioles (stemlets); the edges have very fine teeth. Leaves are 2 to 6 inches long and one-third as wide. The top side is bright green, smooth and glossy, with distinct slightly curving veins; undersides are paler and sometimes slightly hairy.

FRUIT: Round, opaque drupes, ¼ to ⅜ inch in diameter, grow on short, fuzzy stemlets from the leaf axils. Fruits are red most of the summer; most turn black in fall, but red fruits may be present even in fall. The fruit causes digestive upset; most sources consider it inedible.

SEASON: Small, yellowish-white flowers appear in spring. Fruits follow, and are red starting in midsummer; many turn black in fall.

COMPARE: Several other shrubs in our area have quantities of red fruit along the branches; the following pages help distinguish them. Bush honeysuckle (pg. 144) have opposite leaves. Winterberry, catberry and possumhaw (pg. 152) have shorter leaves with a fine network of veins. Fruits and leaves of autumn olive (pg. 154) are dotted with fine silver scales. Leaves of spicebush (pg. 156) and glossy buckthorn (pg. 294) are broader and shorter. Leaves of American holly (pg. 164) have spine-tipped points. Lanceleaf buckthorn (pg. 278) is smaller overall, with smaller leaves.

NOTES: Songbirds eat the fruits; deer browse on the twigs in winter. Some sources list this as *Rhamnus caroliniana*.

green = key identification feature

Bark

LARGE SHRUB
OR SMALL TREE

ALTERNATE
LEAVES

FALL

American Holly

Ilex opaca

HABITAT: This native plant prefers moist, well-drained soils, and is found in mixed-wood forests, especially in hilly areas and near streams; it often grows under tall pines. It does best in sunny areas, but tolerates shade.

GROWTH: Although it can grow as a fairly tall tree, American holly is more frequently seen in the wild as a large shrub or small tree, typically shorter than 40 feet. Twigs are downy and light brown or gray; branches and the main trunk are smooth and gray, often spotted with lichens. American holly plants are unisexual—a plant is either male or female, and each produces a different type of flower. Only female plants bear fruit.

LEAVES: Leathery, glossy evergreen leaves with several widely spaced, spine-tipped points grow alternately on short petioles (stemlets); leaf edges are smooth and untoothed between the points. Leaf bases are tapered, and the tip comes to a sharp, spiny point. Leaves are oval, 1¼ to 4 inches long and half as wide; top sides are deep green, while the undersides are yellowish-green with scattered short hairs (visible with a lens) on the veins.

FRUIT: Firm, round, opaque drupes, ¼ to ½ inch across, grow in clusters from leaf axils of female plants; they are red at maturity. Drupes grow on thin stemlets; each drupe has a small dark spot on the bottom and typically four small, ribbed seeds. The fruits are bitter and mildly toxic to humans, although they are a winter food source for birds and deer.

SEASON: Small, greenish-white flowers develop in mid to late spring; fruits follow, ripening to red in fall. Ripe fruits remain on the plants through winter, making an attractive display with the evergreen leaves.

COMPARE: Winterberry, catberry and possumhaw (pg. 152) are related shrubs with red fruits growing from the leaf axils, but their leaf edges lack the spiny points.

NOTES: The close-grained wood is turned into veneer, and sometimes dyed black to use as an ebony substitute for piano keys, fretboards and inlays. American Indians preserved the fruits to use as buttons.

green = key identification feature

TREE

ALTERNATE
LEAVES

EARLY TO
MID SUMMER

* see below

Mulberries

Morus spp.

HABITAT: Two mulberries inhabit our area: the introduced white mulberry (*Morus alba*), and the less-common native red mulberry (*M. rubra*). Both are found in woodlands, fields, urban areas, and along fencelines and road ditches. White mulberry prefers sun, while red mulberry prefers shade and is found in deeper forests.

GROWTH: Medium to large trees; white mulberry is generally 25 to 40 feet high, while red mulberry can grow to 60 feet. Bark of older trees is brown and ridged; white mulberry bark has **orange-colored areas between the ridges**, while red mulberry bark is uniform in color. White mulberry stems are **pinkish-brown**; red mulberry's are **light tan**.

LEAVES: Alternate, with highly variable shape; some have irregular lobes, appearing **mitten-like**. White mulberry leaves are usually bright green and glossy; they are 3 to 4 inches long with **rounded teeth** on the edges. Red mulberry leaves are usually deep green and dull with hairy undersides; they are up to 10 inches long with **fine, pointed teeth** on the edges.

FRUIT: A multiple fruit up to 1 inch long, composed of numerous drupes originating from a cluster of flowers. A short, soft stemlet remains attached to the picked fruit. Ripe white mulberry fruit may be white, but is more often pink, red or tinged with purple; red mulberries are blackish. Mulberries are sweet, and can be eaten raw or cooked. There are no toxic look-alikes; however, the fruit must be fully ripe and soft before eating, as unripe fruit and all other parts of the plant are mildly toxic.

SEASON: Fruits ripen in early to mid summer.

COMPARE: No tree resembles mulberries that are bearing fruit.

NOTES: Much confusing information exists about the differences between white and red mulberries. The information presented here relies on an excellent paper, *Red and White Mulberry in Indiana* (Sally S. Weeks; Purdue University). It's easy to identify a mulberry, but hard to determine exact species; however, the differences between them are less important to the forager than to the botanist.

green = key identification feature

*combined range

White mulberry tree and fruit

White mulberry bark

DELICIOUS

TREE

ALTERNATE
LEAVES

EARLY TO
MID SUMMER

Sweet

Mahaleb

Sour
* see below

Non-Native Cherries

Prunus spp.

HABITAT: Three non-native cherries may be found scattered in the wild in our area. Sweet cherry (*Prunus avium*) and sour cherry (*P. cerasus*) are cultivated as fruit crops; Mahaleb cherry (*P. mahaleb*) is grown as a rootstock for grafting commercial cherries. All inhabit areas with well-drained soil and abundant sunshine, including old fields and open woods.

GROWTH: All are medium trees, generally 30 feet or less in height. Twigs are tan or greenish; older stems are brownish with bumpy lenticels (breathing pores). The trunk has glossy gray-brown or purplish bark with rough-textured horizontal bands; bark of older trees may split and peel.

LEAVES: Alternate, with long, grooved petioles (stemlets) and toothy edges. Sweet cherry leaves are oval, up to 5¾ inches long and one-half as wide, with sharp tips; sour cherry are similar in shape but a bit smaller. Mahaleb are 1½ to 2¾ inches long and often heart-shaped. Sweet cherry leaves have two (occasionally more) raised, red glands on the petiole below the leaf base; glands may be present on sour cherry leaves but may be on the leaf base rather than the petiole. Sweet cherry leaves have eight or more pairs of veins; sour cherry have seven or fewer.

FRUIT: Smooth-skinned, rounded drupes that grow from leaf axils or knobby shoots along the branches; each contains a single rounded pit. Sweet and sour cherries are up to 1 inch across and are fairly fleshy; Mahaleb are less than ½ inch, with little flesh. Most sweet cherries are deep red to reddish-black, although some cultivars are golden; they are generally sweet enough to eat raw. Sour cherries are bright red, with a tart but pleasant flavor; they are used for cooking. Mahaleb cherries are deep red; they are bitter and are generally not eaten. There are no toxic look-alikes.

SEASON: Fruits ripen in early to mid summer.

COMPARE: American wild plum (pg. 174) has leaves that are similar to sweet cherry, but branches have thorns and the fruit is larger with a dusty bloom.

NOTES: All parts of the cherry tree except ripe, pitted fruit contain toxins and should not be eaten. Cooking or drying eliminates the harmful compound.

green = key identification feature   *specific IN locations not available

Sweet cherry

Mahaleb cherry

Sour cherry

TREE

ALTERNATE
LEAVES

SUMMER
THROUGH FALL

* see below

Crabapples –AND– Apple

Malus spp.

HABITAT: Numerous crabapple varieties grow in the wild throughout our area; they tend to hybridize, and exact identification is difficult. Crabapples (various *Malus* spp.) are found in a variety of habitats, including open woods, thickets, old fields, streambanks, parks and grasslands. Apples (*M. pumila*), originally from Asia, grow in abandoned orchards and on old homestead sites; they are also found where apple cores have been discarded by hikers and in areas where people feed them to wildlife.

GROWTH: Both are small to medium trees, with a rounded crown and many branches; they may be as short as 5 feet, or as tall as 30 feet, generally with equal or greater spread. Young stems are dark reddish-brown, with numerous pale lenticels (breathing pores); older stems are gray and **coarsely textured**. Native crabapples have thorns; some domestic escapees are thornless. Apple trees are thornless.

LEAVES: **Oval leaves**, tapered at both ends, grow alternately on long petioles (stemlets), often in **small clusters** that alternate along the branch; Toringo or Siebold crab (*M. toringo*) also has some **lobed** leaves. Leaves are 1 to 5 inches long, and generally one-third as wide; margins are **toothy**, but the teeth may be rounded or sharp depending on the species.

FRUIT: Both are rounded pomes. Crabapples often have a crown on the base; some, such as Toringo crabs, have an **indented spot** instead. Crabapples grow on a long, thin stemlet; apple stemlets are stubby. Depending on species, crabapples may be yellow, pink or red, and ½ to 1½ inches across. Apples are red, or yellow with an overall red blush; the skin is dotted with pale speckles, and often has coarse brown or yellowish blotches. All crabapples and apples are edible; some are bitter. There are no toxic look-alikes.

SEASON: Both ripen in late summer to fall; crabapples may also ripen earlier.

COMPARE: Hawthorns (pg. 180) have similar fruit, but leaves are coarsely toothed and trees are thornier; fruits are generally oval.

NOTES: Eating quality of crabapples and apples varies from tree to tree, and also between species. Sample a few before harvesting.

green = key identification feature   *combined range; specific locations not available

Crabapple

Toringo crab

Apple

TREE

ALTERNATE
LEAVES

MID TO
LATE SUMMER

Pin Cherry –OR– Fire Cherry

Prunus pensylvanica

HABITAT: Clearings and edges in mixed-wood forests; hillsides; well-drained riverbanks; rock outcroppings. Prefers sunny sites. Pin cherry is one of the first plants to grow after a forest fire, giving rise to one of its common names, fire cherry.

GROWTH: A small native tree, sometimes appearing like a tall shrub; 3 to 25 feet in height, with an open form and a straight trunk. Bark is reddish-brown and smooth, with prominent raised lenticels (breathing pores); bark on older branches often peels off in horizontal strips.

LEAVES: Narrow, sharp-tipped leaves grow alternately from the stems on reddish petioles (stemlets); leaf edges have fine, rounded teeth. Leaves are 3 to 5 inches long, and roughly one-third as wide.

FRUIT: Round, shiny, bright red drupes, about ¼ inch across, grow from reddish stemlets in bunches along the stem. Fruits are translucent when ripe; the large pit can be seen as a shadow in the center of the fruit when the cherries are sunlit. Pin cherries are edible; they're sour when raw but make delicious jelly. There are no toxic look-alikes.

SEASON: Fruits ripen in mid to late summer; the foraging season is usually short because birds relish the cherries and can pick a tree clean of ripe fruit in a short time.

COMPARE: Black cherry (pg. 300) has similar narrow, toothy leaves, but fruits are black when ripe. The midrib of a black cherry leaf has reddish hairs near the base on the lower side; pin cherry leaves are hairless. Common chokecherries (pg. 148) have red fruits, but leaves are much wider. Black cherries and chokecherries grow in racemes (long clusters).

NOTES: Pin cherries have a pit that is large in proportion to the flesh, so pitting them for a pie would be a thankless task; they are usually juiced to prepare jelly. Pin cherry leaves and pits contain hydrocyanic acid, a cyanide-producing compound. The leaves and pits should never be eaten, and care should be taken to avoid crushing cherry pits when juicing the fruits. Cooking or drying eliminates the harmful compound.

green = key identification feature

TREE

ALTERNATE
LEAVES

MID TO
LATE SUMMER

American Wild Plum
Prunus americana

HABITAT: Mixed-wood and hardwood forests, particularly along the edges; pastures, thickets on the edges of cultivated areas, streamsides and hedgerows. Does best in full sun; will tolerate some shade.

GROWTH: A densely branching native tree with a broad crown, up to 25 feet in height with equal spread but often much shorter. Main branches are stiff and dark reddish-brown, with numerous lenticels (breathing pores); many branches are armed with thorns. Older bark is reddish-gray, with a rough texture; it often comes off the tree in large plates.

LEAVES: Oval leaves that taper at both ends are 3 to 4 inches long and roughly one-third as wide; they grow alternately on fairly long petioles (stemlets). Edges are finely toothed; the tip is sharply pointed. Leaves are smooth and deep green above, paler below.

FRUIT: A fleshy, egg-shaped to round drupe with an oval pit, usually about 1 inch across. Fruits have a dusty bloom on the surface, and many have a slight vertical cleft. Ripe fruits are bright reddish-orange to reddish-purple, with juicy, sweet, yellowish flesh. Fruits are edible raw or cooked; tastiness varies from plant to plant. There are no toxic look-alikes.

SEASON: White flowers appear in spring, before the leaves. Fruits ripen from mid through late summer.

COMPARE: Two other thorny plum trees with red fruits inhabit our area. Chickasaw plum (*P. angustifolia*) is a smaller tree, often appearing shrub-like and forming dense thickets; young twigs are reddish and leaves are folded along the midline. Canadian plum (*P. nigra*), a more northern species, has broader leaves; leaf teeth are blunt with small glands (visible with a lens). Mexican plum (pg. 208) is thorny, but ripe fruits are purplish-red. For information on thornless plums, see pg. 176. Peaches (pg. 76) have somewhat similar fruits, but leaves are much longer and narrower.

NOTES: Plum leaves, stems and pits contain hydrocyanic acid, a cyanide-producing compound. The leaves and pits should never be eaten, and care should be taken to avoid crushing plum pits when juicing the fruits.

green = key identification feature

Thorns on trunk

TREE

ALTERNATE
LEAVES

MID TO
LATE SUMMER

Munson's

Hortulan

Goose Plums

Prunus spp.

HABITAT: Two native plums in our area are called goose plum; to distinguish them, they are also called Munson's plum (*Prunus munsoniana*) and Hortulan plum (*P. hortulana*). Both grow in sunny areas with moist, well-drained soil; they are sometimes seen along highways, fencerows and forest edges.

GROWTH: Both grow to 20 feet in height, but are often shorter, shrubby-looking plants growing in dense thickets. Branches are dark brown, with numerous lenticels (breathing pores); older bark is reddish-gray, with a rough texture. Unlike many other wild plums, goose plums are thornless, although Hortulan plum twigs may have a spine on the end.

LEAVES: Elliptical leaves, broadest towards the base, grow alternately on fairly long petioles (stemlets). Leaves are smooth and deep green above, paler below. Edges are finely toothed; the tip is sharply pointed. Leaves of Munson's plum are 2 to 4 inches long and tend to fold along the midline; teeth are rounded and many have visible reddish glands on the underside. Leaves of Hortulan plum are up to 6 inches long, and the teeth are more sharply pointed.

FRUIT: A fleshy, egg-shaped to round drupe, ¾ to 1 inch across with a slight vertical cleft and a flattened oval pit. Ripe Munson's plums are bright red; Hortulan may be red or yellow. Both are edible raw or cooked; tastiness varies from plant to plant. There are no toxic look-alikes.

SEASON: Munson's plum produces masses of white flowers in early spring, before leaves appear. Hortulan plum flowers a bit later, after the leaves have formed. Fruits of both are ripe in mid to late summer.

COMPARE: Some wild plums have thorns; see pgs. 174 and 208.

NOTES: Plum leaves, stems and pits contain hydrocyanic acid, a cyanide-producing compound. The leaves and pits should never be eaten, and care should be taken to avoid crushing plum pits when juicing the fruits. Cooking or drying eliminates the harmful compound.

green = key identification feature

Munson's plum

TREE

OPPOSITE
LEAVES

LATE
SUMMER

Flowering Dogwood

Cornus florida

HABITAT: This native tree is found in areas with cool, moist, well-drained soil; it is common in the understory of hardwood and mixed-wood forests. It prefers ample sunlight, although it will grow in partial shade.

GROWTH: A small tree, typically 25 feet in height or less, with equal or greater width. The tree produces branches fairly close to the ground; they continue up the trunk in a layered fashion. Twigs are green to purplish, and finely hairy; the trunk has dark brownish-gray bark that is broken into square patches, somewhat similar to the persimmon tree (pg. 80). Masses of flowers with four large, white, petal-like bracts appear in spring, before the tree has leafed out.

LEAVES: Oval leaves, 3 to 5 inches long and one-half as wide, grow oppositely on short, grooved petioles (stemlets); the base is tapered and the tip is sharply pointed. Leaves are smooth-edged, or may have very fine teeth (visible with a lens); edges are often slightly wavy. The veins are prominent, curving to follow the leaf edge. Leaves are dark green most of the summer, developing maroon blotches in late summer and turning mottled red in early fall. When a leaf is pulled apart, fine white threads remain between the leaf pieces.

FRUIT: Tight clusters of shiny, bright red, football-shaped drupes grow at the branch tips; each is ⅓ to ½ inch long and one-third as wide. A black floral remnant is present at the tip. The fruit is very bitter when raw; although it is not toxic, most references consider it inedible.

SEASON: Fruits are green in early summer, ripening to red in late summer; they may persist through winter if not eaten by birds.

COMPARE: Leaves of flowering dogwood resemble other members of the *Cornus* family, but with its distinctive flowers, bright red fruits, blocky bark and lovely fall color, flowering dogwood is easy to recognize.

NOTES: The fruits are an important winter food source for birds including quail, waxwings, wild turkeys, robins and cardinals; deer browse on the leaves and twigs.

green = key identification feature

TREE

ALTERNATE
LEAVES

MIDSUMMER
THROUGH FALL

* see below

Hawthorns

Crataegus spp.

HABITAT: Over three dozen species of hawthorn are found in the wild in our area; they hybridize frequently, and identification of exact species in the wild is a matter for specialists. Hawthorns inhabit rocky areas, pastures, old fields and woodlots, sun-dappled mixed-wood forests, and shelter-belts. Trees in sunny areas produce the most fruit.

GROWTH: Small to medium trees, occasionally appearing as large shrubs; height varies wildly, from 6 feet to over 40 feet. Hawthorns often have a rounded crown and widely spreading branches. Thorns—often long and sharp, as in the photo at right—are always present on native wild hawthorns, but may be negligible or absent on cultivated varieties which have escaped into the wild. Bark on the main trunk is usually dark gray and roughly textured, with vertical fissures; young stems are smooth and gray-brown.

LEAVES: Hawthorn leaves are sharply toothed, although specific shape is variable. The most easily identifiable hawthorns have leaves that are broadly tapered and smooth-edged at the base, with coarse, sharp teeth from the end of the base to the tip. Some species have toothy lobes; others are oval, like crabapple leaves but with larger, sharper teeth. Leaves are typically 2 to 4 inches long, and grow alternately.

FRUIT: Pomes, generally oval with slightly flattened sides; they have a crown on the bottom and grow on a long stemlet. Fruits are generally reddish when ripe, but may be yellowish; size ranges from ¼ to 1 inch across. All hawthorns are edible; there are no toxic look-alikes.

SEASON: Hawthorns ripen from midsummer through early fall.

COMPARE: Crabapples (pg. 170) are similar, but leaves are more reliably oval-shaped, with finer, rounded teeth; their fruits are generally rounder.

NOTES: Before harvesting hawthorns, taste a few from the tree you're considering. The best hawthorns have a fair amount of juicy flesh in proportion to the seeds; flesh may be soft and tender, or crunchy like an apple, and the flavor is often reminiscent of pears.

green = key identification feature

*combined range

TREE

ALTERNATE
COMPOUND
LEAVES

LATE SUMMER
THROUGH FALL

Smooth

Staghorn

Smooth Sumac
–AND– Staghorn Sumac

Rhus spp.

HABITAT: These native trees grow in sunny fields and fencerows, disturbed areas, road ditches and embankments, and on waste ground.

GROWTH: Small trees up to 15 feet tall, sometimes appearing as large shrubs. Sumac spreads via rhizomes (underground root-bearing stems), and usually grows in dense colonies. Smooth sumac (*Rhus glabra*) has **smooth twigs and leafstalks**; those of staghorn sumac (*R. typhina*) are covered with **fine, dense hairs**. Bark of both is dark and smooth.

LEAVES: Pinnately (feather-like) compound leaves, each with 11 to 31 leaflets, grow alternately. Leaves are 12 to 24 inches long. Leaflets are 2 to 5 inches long, lance-shaped with toothy edges; deep green on top, paler underneath. Leafstalks of smooth sumac are **reddish**; those of staghorn sumac are **greenish to tan**. Leaves turn red in fall.

FRUIT: Large, **cone-shaped clusters of fuzzy, deep red drupes** grow **upright** at the end of the branches, rising above the leaves. Smooth sumac has clusters that are **irregular**; often, two or three clusters of various sizes grow side-by-side at the end of the branch. Staghorn sumac has a **single, fairly symmetrical cluster** at the end of the branch. Clusters are typically 3 to 6 inches long. The drupes are lemony-sour, and can be used to make a lemonade-type beverage. There are no toxic look-alikes with deep red fruits; however, people who are highly allergic to poison ivy, mangoes or cashews should avoid all sumacs, which are in the same family and may cause a severe allergic reaction.

SEASON: Sumac clusters ripen in late summer, and persist on the plant through winter, although their flavor is washed away by fall rains.

COMPARE: Winged sumac (pg. 206) is similar in overall appearance, but the leafstalk has green wing-like extensions between the leaflets; its fruit clusters are purplish in the summer, ripening to red in fall.

NOTES: Strain sumac lemonade to remove tiny hairs that irritate the throat.

green = key identification feature

Smooth sumac

Staghorn sumac

TREE

ALTERNATE
LEAVES

LATE SUMMER
THROUGH FALL

Cucumber-tree

Umbrella-tree

Cucumber-Tree
–AND– **Umbrella-Tree**
Magnolia spp.

HABITAT: These native trees prefer mountainous or hilly areas with rich, moist, well-drained soil. They are found scattered in well-drained bottomlands, along streambanks and on cool hillsides. They prefer light shade.

GROWTH: Cucumber-tree (*Magnolia acuminata*) is the larger of the two species, attaining heights up to 80 feet; umbrella-tree (*M. tripetala*) grows to 40 feet. The bark of the cucumber-tree is rough and flaky; bark of the umbrella-tree is smooth, with scattered warty lenticels (breathing pores), similar to other magnolias.

LEAVES: Both trees have large, smooth, bright green leaves which are broadly oval, with pointed tips; leaf edges are smooth, and may appear slightly wavy. Cucumber-tree leaves are up to 10 inches long and one-half as wide, growing alternately along the branches on long, fleshy petioles (stemlets); leaf bases are broad. Umbrella-tree leaves are up to 20 inches long and about one-third as wide, growing on petioles in clusters at the ends of the branches; leaf bases are tapered.

FRUIT: Both trees produce a fleshy, inedible fruit that resembles a narrow green pineapple when young. Umbrella-tree fruit is 4 to 6 inches long and stays fairly symmetrical, ripening to pink. Cucumber-tree fruit starts out symmetrical, but quickly becomes misshapen while still green; the ripe, reddish fruit appears swollen and knobby. In fall, both fruits split open to release red seeds; cucumber-tree fruits sometimes do not split to release their seeds, eventually falling to the ground whole.

SEASON: Green fruits are present most of the summer, ripening in late summer to early fall; the fruits split and release seeds in fall.

COMPARE: In our area, two magnolias with similar fruits are found occasionally, primarily in southeastern Kentucky. Bigleaf magnolia (*M. macrophylla*) has leaves up to 30 inches long; those of mountain magnolia (*M. fraseri*) are up to 12 inches long, with rounded lobes at the base.

NOTES: Both of these magnolias are listed as endangered in Indiana.

green = key identification feature

Cucumber-tree (ripe)

Cucumber-tree (green)

Umbrella-tree (ripe)

Umbrella-tree (seeds)

TENDER
LEAFY PLANT

WHORLED
LEAVES

MID TO
LATE SUMMER

Indian Cucumber

Medeola virginiana

HABITAT: This native perennial inhabits open, well-drained areas in moist mixed-wood, coniferous or deciduous forests; also found along edges of bogs and swamps.

GROWTH: A single stem, up to 2½ feet in height, grows from a rhizome (underground root-bearing stem). Most plants have **two whorls of leaves**: a larger whorl about midway up the stem, and a smaller whorl, with fewer leaves, at the top. Smaller plants have only the larger whorl; it sits on top of the stem, which is shorter than the stem on a plant with two whorls. Berries are produced on plants with two whorls.

LEAVES: The large whorl consists of five to nine lance-shaped leaves radiating from the stem. These leaves are 2½ to 4½ inches long and one-third to one-half as wide, tapering to points on both ends. The smaller whorl consists of three to five leaves that are lance-shaped but proportionally broader than those of the lower whorl; these leaves are 1¼ to 2¼ inches long. All leaves have parallel veins and smooth edges; leaf surfaces are smooth and shiny.

FRUIT: Round, glossy, dark purple berries, each ⅛ to ⅓ inch across, **grow on short, erect stemlets** in a cluster from the **center of the upper whorl**; stemlets are red when the berries are ripe. The berries are inedible.

SEASON: Yellow flowers bloom in early summer; berries follow and are ripe from mid to late summer. The leaves have usually yellowed and withered by the time the fruit is ripe.

COMPARE: Several plants in our area have similar whorled leaves, but their fruits are different. Black snakeroot (*Sanicula marilandica*) has two tiers of whorled leaves, but it produces a pod, not berries. Starflower (*Trientalis borealis*) and whorled pogonia (*Isotria verticillata* and *I. medeoloides*) have a single whorl; their fruits are dry capsules. Bunchberry (pg. 92) often appears to have similar whorled leaves, but its fruits are red.

NOTES: The rhizome of Indian cucumber can be eaten; it has a cucumber-like taste, giving the plant its common name.

green = key identification feature

Unripe berries

Ripe berries

TENDER
LEAFY PLANT

ALTERNATE
COMPOUND
LEAVES

LATE SUMMER
TO FALL

American Spikenard

Aralia racemosa

HABITAT: This native plant is found in rich, open deciduous and mixed-wood forests, thickets, wooded slopes and ravines. It prefers moist, well-drained soil, and grows in full sun to part shade.

GROWTH: A **very large, bushy**, somewhat top-heavy plant that is almost shrublike and grows from a rhizome (an underground root-bearing stem). Typically 3 to 5 feet in height, with equal width near the top; white flowers grow in **numerous long, loose, upright clusters** that have an overall conical shape. Stems are soft and greenish-purple, with fine hairs.

LEAVES: Large doubly compound leaves, each with three divisions, grow alternately on the stems; overall leaf length is up to 3 feet. Each of the three divisions has three to five heart-shaped leaflets that are 3 to 6 inches long and two-thirds as wide, with doubly toothed edges and a pointed tip. Leaflets are green and slightly hairy on both surfaces; leaflet nodes are often purplish.

FRUIT: Round drupes, each up to ¼ inch across, replace the flowers in the long, loose clusters (racemes); drupes are greenish when young, ripening to reddish-purple. The effect is that of a **long column of tiny grapes**. The fruits have a sharp, unpleasant aftertaste; although a few sources list them as edible, most say they should not be eaten.

SEASON: Spikenard flowers in mid to late summer; fruits ripen from late summer to fall.

COMPARE: A related plant, bristly sarsaparilla (*A. hispida*), is found in our area only in northernmost Indiana and extreme northeastern Ohio. It is smaller overall, with much smaller leaves; its lower stems are covered with stiff, bristly hairs. Its fruits are larger and black, and grow in rounded clusters rather than long racemes. All parts of the plant have an unpleasant odor. Fruits of bristly sarsaparilla are generally regarded as inedible.

NOTES: Like the related sarsaparilla (pg. 242), spikenard has aromatic, spicy-flavored rhizomes that are used as a flavoring agent, and can also be eaten when cooked. Young shoot tips can also be cooked as a vegetable.

green = key identification feature

WOODY VINE

ALTERNATE LEAVES

LATE SUMMER TO EARLY FALL

Riverbank

Summer

Fox

Purple Wild Grapes

Vitis spp.

HABITAT: Moist, rich areas with ample sun including thickets, clearings, open woods, river and streambanks and woodland margins.

GROWTH: The three grapes discussed here are native woody vines with flexible stems and purplish fruits; they have shreddy bark and use forked tendrils to climb. Riverbank grapes (*Vitis riparia*) climb as high as 70 feet. Summer grapes (*V. aestivalis;* also called pigeon grapes) and fox grapes (*V. labrusca*) are generally 35 feet or less.

LEAVES: Toothy leaves grow alternately on long petioles (stemlets). Leaves are heart-shaped, usually with shallow or indistinct lobes; summer and fox grape vines may have a few deeply lobed leaves. Teeth on riverbank leaves are coarse and sharp, while those of summer and fox grape are finer and often rounded; fox grape leaves usually have tiny points along the edge. Riverbank petioles are less than 2 inches long; summer and fox grape petioles are longer. Summer and fox grape leaves are white or whitish-tan below; fox grape leaves are thick and leathery.

FRUIT: Clusters of edible round, juicy berries hang from the vine on separate stalks, opposite a leaf; each grape has one to several teardrop-shaped seeds. Riverbank grapes are ⅜ to ½ inch across and bluish-purple with a heavy whitish bloom; they grow in large, tight clusters. Summer grapes are ¼ to ⅜ inch across and reddish- or bluish-purple with a medium bloom, turning purplish-black in early fall; clusters are large and often loose. Fox grapes are ½ to ¾ inch across and dark purple with a slight bloom; clusters are small, usually with 15 or fewer grapes in each.

SEASON: The grapes listed here ripen in late summer to early fall.

COMPARE: Several species of grapes in our area have blackish fruits (pg. 254). Muscadine (pg. 192) has large purplish-red to purplish-black fruits; some are bronze. Wild grapes may be confused with several inedible or toxic fruits; please see "Be certain, be safe: Wild grapes" on pg. 20.

NOTES: Another wild grape, *V. vulpina* (pg. 254) is also occasionally called fox grape; that common name is used here for *V. labrusca*.

green = key identification feature

Riverbank grapes

Fox grapes

Summer grape leaves, immature fruit

WOODY VINE

ALTERNATE LEAVES

LATE SUMMER TO EARLY FALL

Muscadine

Vitis rotundifolia

HABITAT: This native grape is an aggressive plant, common in the southeastern United States; Kentucky is in the northern part of its range. It is found in open forests, and along paths and streams. It does best in areas with moderate moisture and produces more fruit when it receives ample sun.

GROWTH: A stout, woody vine that uses tendrils to climb; may grow as long as 100 feet. On native muscadines, tendrils are unbranched rather than forked; hybrids between native muscadines and other grapes may also be found in the wild, and these have forked tendrils. Young stems are slightly angled and have bumpy lenticels (breathing pores). The bark on the trunk is smooth and does not shred off in strips like other grapes, although very old, large muscadine trunks develop flaky vertical ridges.

LEAVES: Heart-shaped leaves with large teeth on the edges grow alternately on long petioles (stemlets); the leaves may have shallow lobes or no lobes, and sometimes appear round except for the notch at the base. Leaves are 2 to 5 inches wide and nearly as long; they are shiny, bright green on top and yellowish-green underneath.

FRUIT: Small clusters of edible round berries hang from the vine on separate stalks, opposite a leaf; each grape has one to five large teardrop-shaped seeds. Our largest wild grape, muscadines are up to 1 inch across. Ripe fruit is typically purplish-red to purplish-black but may also be bronze-colored; they lack the whitish bloom found on many other wild grapes, and are usually speckled. The skin is tough, but the flesh is juicy and sweet, with a musky but fruity flavor. Unlike other grapes, muscadines ripen individually and fall off soon after ripening. Picked fruits spoil easily because the skin has a large break where it was attached to the stemlet.

SEASON: Immature fruits are green, ripening in late summer to early fall.

COMPARE: Several grapes in our area have purplish fruits (pg. 190); others are blackish (pg. 254). Wild grapes may be confused with several inedible or toxic fruits; please see "Be certain, be safe: Wild grapes" on pg. 20.

NOTES: Muscadine cultivars are frequently grown commercially.

green = key identification feature

Muscadine trunks (on left) next to water oak

WOODY
VINE

ALTERNATE
LEAVES

LATE SUMMER
TO EARLY FALL

Canada Moonseed

Menispermum canadense

HABITAT: Streambanks, thickets, moist woody areas. Prefers full sun.

GROWTH: This native woody vine reaches up to 20 feet in length. Unlike wild grapes, moonseed has **no tendrils**, and climbs by coiling its central stem around the supporting plant or structure. Younger stems are hairy, greenish or reddish and flexible; older stems are smooth, bronze to dark reddish-brown and woody.

LEAVES: Alternate, with three to seven shallow lobes; edges are **smooth and untoothed**. The long petiole (stemlet) is attached to the underside of the leaf, **slightly away from the base** (peltate). The upper surface is smooth and light green; the underside is silvery-green with fine hairs. Leaves are 4 to 7 inches long, and equally wide.

FRUIT: Purplish-blue to purplish-black drupes with a whitish bloom, each containing a **single flat seed shaped like a broad crescent** (a circle with a bite taken away). Drupes are round and ¼ to ⅓ inch across; they grow in **loose clusters** that hang from the vine on a **long, spindly fruit stalk**, opposite a leaf. They are **highly toxic**.

SEASON: Moonseed fruits are ripe in late summer to early fall, at about the same time as wild grapes.

COMPARE: Moonseed bears an unfortunate resemblance to some species of wild grapes (pgs. 190, 192, 254). However, the leaves of wild grapes have toothy edges, and are attached directly to the petiole; those of moonseed have smooth edges and peltate attachment. Grapes have one to six small, oval or pear-shaped seeds, rather than the single crescent-shaped seed that gives moonseed its common name. Finally, grapes attach themselves to hosts by using tendrils, which are absent on moonseed. It is very important to pay strict attention when harvesting wild grapes, to avoid gathering any moonseed fruits, which are toxic.

NOTES: Moonseed fruits contain the alkaloid dauricine, a compound that affects the heart. Its use in medicine is being studied, but it is toxic in its natural form as found in moonseed.

green = key identification feature

Fruits and seed

WOODY
VINE

ALTERNATE
LEAVES

LATE SUMMER
THROUGH FALL

Heartleaf Peppervine –OR–
Raccoon Grape

Ampelopsis cordata

HABITAT: This native woody vine is found in rich, moist, well-drained areas including river and streambanks, alongside highways and rural roads, woodland margins, pond edges and waste ground. It grows in sun or partial shade.

GROWTH: A vining plant that can grow to 60 feet in length; it uses its occasional branched tendrils and a twining habit to climb other plants, fences, poles or buildings. Young stems are green and flexible, with slightly angled edges; older stems are brown and woody, with raised, bumpy lenticels (breathing pores). The trunk is often several inches in diameter; it has non-shredding brown bark with long ridges.

LEAVES: Heart-shaped leaves with a broad, flat base grow alternately from the vine on a petiole (stemlet) that is almost as long as the leaf. Edges have coarse, sharp teeth. Leaves are up to 5 inches long, and nearly as wide at the base; the tip is sharply pointed.

FRUIT: Loose, wide clusters of speckled berries hang from the vine on a thin fruit stalk, opposite a leaf. Berries are about ¼ inch across and are round or slightly flattened; they may be maroon, purple, blue, orangish or pink—all on the same plant, at the same time. The fruits are inedible.

SEASON: Berries mature from late summer through fall.

COMPARE: Porcelainberry (*A. brevipedunculata*) is a non-native woody vine with similarly multicolored fruits growing in loose clusters, but its leaves are deeply lobed. In our area, it is found scattered in a few counties in Ohio and Kentucky. Porcelainberry and heartleaf peppervine both have some similarities to wild grapes (pgs. 190, 192, 254), but grapes grow in tighter, longer clusters; the fruits are not multicolored, stems have no lenticels and bark of all grapes except muscadine (pg. 192) is shreddy.

NOTES: Heartleaf peppervine and porcelainberry are considered weedy, nuisance plants. Birds eat the berries, helping to spread the plants.

green = key identification feature

Porcelainberry

SMALL
WOODY SHRUB

ALTERNATE
LEAVES

MID TO
LATE SUMMER

Prickly

Smooth

Prickly Gooseberry –AND–
Smooth Gooseberry

Ribes spp.

HABITAT: Two native gooseberry shrubs with purplish fruits grow in our area. Prickly or pasture gooseberry (*Ribes cynosbati*) is found in thickets and tangled areas; it also grows in rich, moist woods and rocky areas, especially those along rivers or ponds. Smooth or swamp gooseberry (*R. hirtellum*) is found in similar locations, but also grows in boggy areas.

GROWTH: Both are arching shrubs about 3 feet high. Leaf nodes have one to three thorns; prickly gooseberry thorns are fairly weak, while those of smooth gooseberry are stout. Prickly gooseberry stems have scattered bristles, especially on younger growth; smooth gooseberry stems have fine hairs but no bristles, although young stems have small prickles.

LEAVES: Attached alternately to the stem by a petiole (stemlet); each leaf node has one to three leaves. Each leaf has three to five distinct lobes, resembling a maple leaf with rounded teeth.

FRUIT: The ¼- to ½-inch round berry grows on a thin stemlet from leaf nodes, singly or in small clusters. Distinct stripes run longitudinally on the berry; a prominent flower remnant, often called a pigtail, is present at the end of the berry. Prickly gooseberries have soft prickles, either overall or on the half of the fruit closest to the stem; ripe fruits are reddish-purple. Smooth gooseberries are smooth and purple or purplish-black when ripe. Gooseberries are edible in both the green and ripe stages.

SEASON: Ripe fruits are present from mid to late summer.

COMPARE: Fruits of Missouri gooseberry (pg. 266) have smooth skins and are black when ripe; stems have scattered thin bristles. Currant shrubs (pgs. 128, 268) resemble gooseberry shrubs, but berries are smaller and typically grow in racemes (long clusters of multiple fruits).

NOTES: Ripe gooseberries are excellent in baked desserts, sauces and other dishes. Green gooseberries (pg. 48) are rich in pectin, and are used for jam and jelly. Prickly gooseberries are not eaten raw due to the prickles.

green = key identification feature

Prickly gooseberry

Smooth gooseberry

LARGE
WOODY SHRUB

OPPOSITE
COMPOUND
LEAVES

MID TO
LATE SUMMER

Common Elderberry
Sambucus canadensis

HABITAT: This native shrub grows in moist areas such as river and stream-banks, woodland edges, shelterbelts, thickets, abandoned fields, road-sides, meadows, and ditch edges. It prefers full sun to part shade.

GROWTH: An open shrub, 5 to 12 feet in height, with a broad, rounded crown. Branches are yellowish-gray, with numerous warty lenticels (breathing pores); older bark is yellowish-brown or gray, streaked with white. White flowers grow in large, showy umbrella-like clusters; stemlets are reddish. When the flowers fall and berries are developing, the plant is easy to spot because of the **groupings of rounded, reddish-purple flower stemlets**, which have a **lacy appearance**.

LEAVES: Compound leaves, each with 5 to 11 leaflets, grow oppositely on the stem; leaves are 6 to 10 inches long and nearly as wide. Leaflets are 2 to 4 inches long and one-half as wide, broadly oval and tapered on both ends; edges are sharply toothed. The top sides are dark green and smooth; the undersides are paler and may be downy.

FRUIT: Round berries, about ³⁄₁₆ inch in diameter with three to five seeds, grow in **drooping, flat-topped clusters** (cymes). Berries are green when immature, ripening to **deep purple or purplish-black**; berry stemlets are reddish-purple. The berries are edible, and are juiced to make jelly, jam and wine. Leaves, stems, seeds and all other parts of all elderberry species are toxic. Common elderberry might be confused with red elderberry (pg. 142). See below for more information about this plant; its berries are generally not eaten.

SEASON: Flowers appear in early summer; fruits ripen in mid to late summer.

COMPARE: Red elderberry (pg. 142) has similar growth and leaves, but berries are bright red and grow in rounded clusters, rather than the flat-topped clusters of common elderberry. Red elderberry ripens a month or more before common elderberry; its fruits are regarded as inedible.

NOTES: Some sources list this plant as *Sambucus nigra* ssp. *canadensis*. The flowers are used to make wine, and also a tea to treat headache.

green = key identification feature

LARGE SHRUB
OR SMALL TREE

OPPOSITE
LEAVES

EARLY
SUMMER

Eastern Swamp Privet

Forestiera acuminata

HABITAT: Low, wet areas such as swamps, sloughs, bottomland forests and bayous; also found along streams, lakes and ponds. It grows in areas with full sun to moderate shade, and can survive sustained flooding during the growing season.

GROWTH: This native plant is a large shrub or small tree, up to 30 feet in height but usually shorter. It has an unkempt, straggly appearance, with an open crown. Young branches are smooth and light brown, with numerous pale lenticels (breathing pores); twig tips sometimes have a **spine at the end.** Older branches are gray; the trunk has dark brown bark that is smooth or slightly ridged. Swamp privet is usually unisexual—a plant is either male or female, and each produces a different type of flower. Typically, only female plants bear fruit.

LEAVES: Glossy, smooth, yellowish-green leaves, 2 to 4 inches long and one-half as wide, grow oppositely on ½-inch petioles (stemlets) that have **flattened edges.** The leaves are widest at the midpoint, with a **sharply pointed tip** and a base that tapers to a V; the overall impression is that of a **round-sided diamond.** Edges are slightly toothy above the midpoint. The undersides are pale and have scattered fine hairs on the veins.

FRUIT: An elongated, lightly textured oval drupe, up to ¾ inch long, that is purple or purplish-black when ripe. A few sources consider the fruits edible; however, the drupes are very thin-fleshed and are generally regarded as inedible.

SEASON: Masses of yellow flowers appear in spring, before the plants have leafed out. Fruits develop in late spring; they ripen in early summer and often fall off the plant, or are eaten by birds, shortly after.

COMPARE: Upland swamp privet (*F. ligustrina*) is a southeastern species; in our area, it is found only occasionally in southern Kentucky, where it is listed as threatened. Its leaves are smaller and lack the sharp tip of eastern swamp privet; it inhabits dry, rocky areas.

NOTES: The fruits are relished by waterfowl and other birds.

green = key identification feature

Eastern swamp
privet, ripe fruit

Upland swamp privet

LARGE SHRUB
OR SMALL TREE

ALTERNATE
LEAVES

EARLY TO
MID SUMMER

* see below

Serviceberries
Amelanchier spp.

HABITAT: Six serviceberry varieties are native to our area; all produce edible fruits which look similar. Found in mixed-wood forests and thickets. They may grow as a single specimen, or in groups. Low serviceberry (*Amelanchier humilis*; also called shadbush) and running serviceberry (*A. stolonifera*) spread by runners (horizontal stems) and form colonies; running serviceberry is more likely to grow on **extremely rocky areas**.

GROWTH: An erect shrub or small tree, usually 3 to 15 feet tall; smooth serviceberry (*A. laevis*) may grow to **30 feet**. Bark is smooth, and usually gray or brownish; older bark may have vertical furrows. Roundleaf serviceberry (*A. sanguinea*) has **reddish twigs and branches**.

LEAVES: Alternate, 1 to 3 inches long, with long petioles (stemlets). Leaf edges of running, smooth, downy (*A. arborea*) and inland (*A. interior*) are **finely toothed**; running has leaves that are nearly circular and lack teeth on the bottom half, while smooth, downy and inland leaves are **heart-shaped**. Inland has a very short pointed tip, while the pointed tips on smooth and downy are long. Downy is **densely hairy** underneath, particularly on young leaves. Low serviceberry leaves have coarse teeth on the upper half; roundleaf has coarse teeth around the entire leaf, which is nearly circular.

FRUIT: A ½-inch round pome with a **crown on the base**, resembling a blueberry or a tiny apple, on a long stemlet; fruits grow along a separate fruiting stalk and have a whitish bloom. Most are sweet and delicious; the tiny, soft seeds are unnoticeable. Ripe fruits range from reddish-purple to bluish-purple to black; judge ripeness by texture, and choose soft fruits to harvest. There are no toxic look-alikes.

SEASON: Fruits are ripe from early to mid summer, depending on species and location.

COMPARE: Chokecherries (pg. 148) have similar leaves, but the fruits are smaller and translucent, with no crown on the base.

NOTES: Also called Juneberry, a reference to its blooming time.

green = key identification feature

*combined range

LARGE SHRUB
OR SMALL TREE

ALTERNATE
COMPOUND
LEAVES

LATE SUMMER
THROUGH FALL

Winged –OR– Shining Sumac

Rhus copallinum

HABITAT: This native plant is found in old fields and disturbed areas, along-side roads, in open woods and sandy areas, and on rocky outcrops. It prefers sun, and can tolerate drought. Some sources list it as *R. copallina*.

GROWTH: A large, open shrub or small tree, ranging from 3 to 20 feet in height. Sumac spreads readily via rhizomes (underground root-bearing stems), and is usually seen in dense colonies. Twigs are reddish-brown to gray, with numerous lenticels (breathing pores); young twigs are downy. Older bark is gray to brown, with a rough texture. Dense clusters of tiny yellowish flowers grow upright from the end of the branch; the flowers are present from late spring through late summer.

LEAVES: Pinnately (feather-like) compound leaves, each with 7 to 15 leaf-lets (some accounts say up to 23), grow alternately. Leaves are up to 12 inches long. Leaflets are 1 to 3 inches long and lance-shaped; they are **glossy** and deep green on top, paler and downy underneath. Edges are typically smooth, although some fine teeth may be present. Leafstalks have **flat, wing-like green extensions between the leaflets.** Leaves turn brilliant red in fall.

FRUIT: **Cone-shaped clusters of fuzzy, sticky purplish or pink drupes** develop at the end of the branches starting in midsummer; fruits turn deep maroon in late summer to fall. Clusters are 3 to 5 inches long and often **droop** or hang down The drupes are lemony-sour, and can be used to make a lemonade-type beverage. There are no toxic look-alikes that have purplish, pink or red fruits; however, people who are highly allergic to poison ivy, mangoes, or cashews should avoid all sumacs, which are in the same family and may cause a severe allergic reaction.

SEASON: Sumac clusters ripen in late summer through fall, and persist on the plant through winter; their flavor is washed away by fall rains.

COMPARE: Smooth and staghorn sumac (pg. 182) are similar, but leafstalks lack the wings; fruits are deep red and the fruit clusters stand upright.

NOTES: Strain sumac lemonade to remove tiny hairs that irritate the throat.

green = key identification feature

Fully ripe cluster

TREE

ALTERNATE
LEAVES

LATE
SUMMER

* see below

Mexican Plum

Prunus mexicana

HABITAT: This native plum is found in areas with rich, moist soil, including roadsides, pastures, river bottoms, streamsides and hedgerows. It does best in full sun, but will tolerate some shade.

GROWTH: A medium-sized tree, up to 30 feet in height with equal spread; unlike many other wild plums, it does not form thickets. Branches are smooth and reddish-brown, with numerous lenticels (breathing pores); many branches become **thorny** as they mature. Older bark is gray, with a **rough texture**; it often comes off the tree in **curled strips**, revealing orangish wood underneath.

LEAVES: Oval, **broadest around the midpoint**, up to 5 inches long and one-half as wide. Leaves grow alternately on fairly long petioles (stemlets) which are **densely hairy** on emerging leaves. Leaf edges have fairly fine teeth; the tip is sharply pointed. Leaves are smooth and deep green above, paler below; veins on the underside are hairy.

FRUIT: A fleshy, round to egg-shaped drupe, typically about 1 inch long. Fruits have a **dusty bloom** on the surface, and many have a **slight vertical cleft**. Ripe fruits are **purplish-red**, with juicy, sweet, yellowish flesh. Fruits are edible raw or cooked; tastiness varies from plant to plant. There are no toxic look-alikes.

SEASON: Fragrant white flowers bloom in profusion in early spring, before the leaves appear. Fruits are yellow when immature, turning mauve and finally ripening to purplish-red in late summer.

COMPARE: Several other thorny plum trees, including the common American wild plum (pg. 174), grow in our area, but their ripe fruits are reddish-orange to reddish-purple; see pg. 174 for more information. Goose plums (pg. 176) are thornless; ripe fruits are red or yellow.

NOTES: Plum leaves, stems and pits contain hydrocyanic acid, a cyanide-producing compound. The leaves and pits should never be eaten, and care should be taken to avoid crushing plum pits when juicing the fruits. Cooking or drying eliminates the harmful compounds.

green = key identification feature   *specific KY and OH locations not available

TENDER
LEAFY PLANT

ALTERNATE
LEAVES

MID TO
LATE SUMMER

Smooth Solomon's Seal

Polygonatum biflorum

HABITAT: Rich, moist mixed-wood and deciduous forests, waste ground, urban areas, roadside ditches, thickets, edges of streams and ponds.

GROWTH: This native plant grows as a single stem in a long arch from a rhizome (an underground root-bearing stem). Smooth Solomon's seal is the largest of the Solomon's seal family, and is often called great Solomon's seal because of its size. The stem can grow up to 5 feet in length, although it is usually much shorter; longer stems arch gracefully, making the plant appear shorter than it is.

LEAVES: Lance-shaped leaves with many parallel veins grow alternately, attached directly to the stem or slightly clasping; leaves are 2 to 7 inches long and are typically narrow. Topsides are green and smooth; undersides are paler, with hairless veins. Leaves are broadest near the base, tapering to a point; edges are smooth and hairless.

FRUIT: Round, dark blue berries, about ⅓ inch across with a slight vertical cleft, grow in small groups or singly from the leaf axils. Berries have a slight bloom, and grow from thin stemlets. They are inedible.

SEASON: Berries mature in mid to late summer.

COMPARE: The only other "true" Solomon's seal that grows in our area is hairy Solomon's seal (*P. pubescens*). Like smooth Solomon's seal, berries of hairy Solomon's seal grow from the leaf axils; however, the plant is shorter, generally 3 feet or less in length, and leaves grow on short petioles (stemlets); edges of the leaf, and leaf veins on the undersides, have fine hairs, and there are only one to four berries at each leaf axil. All other Solomon's seals in our area are "false," having the berries growing from the tip of the stem. Please see the common false Solomon's seal text on pg. 100 for more information about plants with similar appearance.

NOTES: The rhizome of smooth Solomon's seal is edible when cooked; however, the plant is protected in much of its range and the rhizome should be harvested only where abundant (and legal).

green = key identification feature

Overview of plant

TENDER
LEAFY PLANT

OPPOSITE
COMPOUND
LEAVES

MID TO
LATE SUMMER

Blue Cohosh
Caulophyllum thalictroides

HABITAT: Rich, moist mixed-wood and deciduous forests, valleys, river bottoms and floodplains. Grows best in shade or dappled sun.

GROWTH: A leafy, native plant that grows from a rhizome (an underground root-bearing stem). The main stem divides into two stems, each with compound leaves that are sub-divided into three stalks. Stalks on the lower leaf each have three to nine leaflets. The upper leaf is smaller; each stalk typically has three leaflets. A separate, leafless flowering stalk rises above the leaves. Blue cohosh is typically 12 to 18 inches in height, but it can reach 3 feet. It often forms colonies.

LEAVES: Blue cohosh has many leaves, growing in a complex pattern as described above. Individual leaflets are typically **tulip-shaped** and have rounded lobes ending in a shallow point, generally three lobes per leaflet but sometimes two. Leaves are up to 12 inches long; individual leaflets are 1 to 3 inches long and often as wide.

FRUIT: What appears to be a berry is actually the seed of the plant; it is round and covered by a thinly fleshy, deep-blue coat with a powdery bloom. Each is about ⅜ inch across; the stemlet is thin and green where it joins the flowering stalk, **thickening where it joins the seed** to somewhat resemble a **tiny blue light bulb**. The seeds are generally regarded as toxic, but some sources report that they can be roasted and used as a coffee substitute.

SEASON: Seeds have a greenish coat in early summer; the coat turns blue in mid to late summer.

COMPARE: Giant blue cohosh (*C. giganteum*), is similar but slightly larger; it has fewer flowers and, therefore, fewer fruits, and is less common. Although neither of the blue cohosh species resembles blueberries, care should be taken when in the woods with children, who may mistake the highly visible blue-coated seeds of blue cohosh as the edible blueberry.

NOTES: Blue cohosh root has been used medicinally to induce labor, and to treat various other gynecological conditions.

green = key identification feature

WOODY
VINE

ALTERNATE
COMPOUND
LEAVES

LATE SUMMER
TO EARLY FALL

Virginia Creeper

Parthenocissus quinquefolia

HABITAT: Moist, well-drained areas including forest edges, cliff bases, streambanks, fencerows, ravines and urban areas. Prefers sun.

GROWTH: A sprawling, native vine that uses sucker-foot tendrils with many branches to attach itself to fences, buildings, walls and other plants, Virginia creeper can grow to 50 feet in length. Older stems at the base of the plant are tan, with rough, shreddy bark; young stems are tan or reddish, with light-colored lenticels (breathing pores).

LEAVES: The palmately compound, shiny leaves typically have five leaflets (occasionally three or seven); they average 7 inches across and grow alternately on long petioles (stemlets) which are often reddish or purplish. Leaflets are oval with tapering ends and a pointed tip; edges above the base are sharply toothed. Generally, two leaflets are much smaller than the others. Leaves are bright green above, paler below; they turn bright scarlet in early fall.

FRUIT: Round berries, about ¼ inch across, grow in loose, open clusters on bright pink stemlets originating opposite a leaf. Ripe berries are deep bluish-purple with a dusty bloom. Many sources list the berries as toxic; others say they are edible but not tasty. They contain calcium oxalate, which may irritate the throat (Mike Krebill). It's best to avoid them.

SEASON: Berries ripen in late summer to early fall, and may persist on the plant after the leaves drop in the fall.

COMPARE: Berries resemble wild grapes (pgs. 190, 192, 254); the resemblance is unfortunate, because these two plants often grow together. The hot-pink berry stemlets and palmately compound leaves make Virginia creeper easy to identify and avoid. Woodbine (*P. vitacea*) is related, and very similar; however, its tendrils have only a few branches and usually lack sucker-feet, fruits are slightly larger and leaves are slightly smaller. In our area, woodbine is found mostly in the northern half of Indiana.

NOTES: Virginia creeper is the larval host of the Virginia creeper sphinx moth. The berries are eaten by many species of birds.

green = key identification feature

Fall leaf color

TENDER
VINE

ALTERNATE
LEAVES

LATE SUMMER
TO EARLY FALL

Yellow Passionflower

Passiflora lutea

HABITAT: This native vine is found in areas with moist, well-drained soil including open woods, thickets, roadsides and railroad embankments. It prefers sunny areas, but will tolerate partial shade.

GROWTH: A non-woody vine up to 15 feet in length, passionflower uses **tendrils** to twine itself around other plants, fences and buildings; if a supporting structure is not present, it will sprawl along the ground. Stems are slightly hairy. Distinctive **yellowish-green, frilly flowers**, ¾ to 1 inch across, grow throughout the summer from leaf axils.

LEAVES: **Broad, three-lobed** leaves grow alternately from 1½- to 2-inch-long petioles (stemlets). Leaves are generally 2 to 5 inches in width, and about two-thirds as long. The lobes are distinct but **fairly shallow**, with rounded tips; the central lobe is sometimes longer than the side lobes. The top surface is dull green, occasionally mottled with lighter patches; the underside is paler. Edges are smooth and untoothed.

FRUIT: Round or egg-shaped berries, typically ½ to ¾ inch long, are green when immature, ripening to **deep blue with a dusty bloom**. Berries grow on long stemlets from leaf axils, and have a **thickened collar** where they are joined to the stemlet. They are filled with numerous small seeds surrounded by gel-like pulp. The seedy pulp is edible, but the fruits are so small that they are generally not gathered by foragers.

SEASON: Flowers are present from mid to late summer; fruits ripen from late summer through early fall.

COMPARE: Purple passionflower (pg. 44) is a similar vine which grows much more aggressively; it has deeply lobed leaves and larger purple flowers, and its ripe fruits are large and green. Yellow passionflower leaves somewhat resemble those of Canada moonseed (pg. 194), but moonseed has no tendrils; the leaf stalk is attached slightly away from the base of the leaf (peltate).

NOTES: The flowers attract numerous species of butterflies and bees; the berries are eaten by birds and small mammals.

green = key identification feature

Yellow passionflower
climbing in loblolly pine

SMALL
WOODY SHRUB

ALTERNATE
LEAVES

MID TO
LATE SUMMER

Blue Ridge

Lowbush

Blue Ridge Blueberry –AND–
Lowbush Blueberry

Vaccinium spp.

HABITAT: Rocky or gravelly areas on the edges of coniferous and mixed-wood forests; clearings; along footpaths; sunny hilltops and ridges. Blueberries are one of the first plants to appear after a forest fire.

GROWTH: Two types of native low-growing blueberries are found in our area: Blue Ridge blueberry (*Vaccinium pallidum*, sometimes listed as *V. vacillans*) and lowbush blueberry (*V. angustifolium*), sometimes called sweet lowbush blueberry. Both are sprawling, woody shrubs that typically grow in spreading colonies. Blue Ridge blueberries are **2 to 3 feet in height**. Lowbush blueberries are shorter, usually about 1 foot in height or less; they tend to hug the ground.

LEAVES: Alternate, oval leaves taper on both ends; edges have very fine teeth, and the tip is a slightly rounded point. Leaves are deep green to bluish-green, turning red in fall; both surfaces are smooth. Blue Ridge leaves are 1 to 2 inches long and half as wide, with whitish undersides; leaves of lowbush blueberries are ½ to 1 inch long and one-third as wide, and are sometimes tinged with red well before fall leaf color appears.

FRUIT: Round berries with a **prominent five-pointed crown** on the bottom; when ripe, they are blue with a **dusty bloom**. Berries are ¼ to ½ inch across, with **small, soft seeds**; they grow in clusters on short stemlets. Ripe berries are delicious raw or cooked. Although there are other plants with berries that are blue, there are no toxic look-alikes as long as good identification practices are followed.

SEASON: Berries ripen in mid to late summer.

COMPARE: Highbush blueberries (pg. 224) are up to 12 feet in height; fruits are very similar. Huckleberries (pg. 270) are slightly taller than Blue Ridge blueberries, with larger leaves. Their fruits are less bloomy and are black-ish when ripe; they are edible, although their seeds are more noticeable.

NOTES: Always look for the crown on the bottom when picking blueberries.

green = key identification feature

Blue Ridge blueberries

Lowbush blueberries

SMALL
WOODY SHRUB

ALTERNATE
LEAVES

LATE
SUMMER

Common Juniper

Juniperus communis

HABITAT: Dry, sunny openings in mixed-wood and coniferous forests; also found on rocky outcrops, ridges and exposed slopes.

GROWTH: In our area, common juniper is a **sprawling evergreen shrub**, up to 4 feet in height, with short branches that tend to grow upright. It can also grow as a tree, but that form is not generally found in our area. Bark is reddish-brown, fibrous and shreddy. Common juniper is unisexual—a plant is either male or female, and each produces a different type of fruit.

LEAVES: Narrow, pointed, awl-like evergreen needles, about ½ inch long, grow alternately in clusters of three; they have a strong smell which is both piney and resinous. Needles are **concave on top, with a whitish center**; undersides are dark green. Except near the tip of the branch, needles usually grow almost perpendicular to the branches, giving each branch a bushy appearance.

FRUIT: The female fruit is a round, berry-like cone, about ⅓ inch across, that grows on a short stemlet or is connected directly to the branch. Cones are **bluish-white, with a waxy bloom**; they are usually profuse. When crushed, they **smell like gin**. (The male fruit, a short catkin, is borne on separate plants.) The cones are used as a seasoning.

SEASON: Fruits ripen in late summer, and usually persist through winter.

COMPARE: Eastern red cedar (pg. 236) is a large tree with similar-looking dusty blue, rounded fruits, but its leaves appear scaly; although its fruits are similar in appearance to common juniper, they are not edible.

NOTES: Common juniper is the most widespread conifer in the world, although it is listed as threatened in Kentucky and endangered in Ohio. It is native to the United States and Canada, as well as Eurasia, Japan, Croatia and Sweden; it typically grows as a columnar tree in areas other than North America, although the tree form is found in New England. The cones of common juniper are used to flavor gin.

green = key identification feature

LARGE
WOODY SHRUB

OPPOSITE
LEAVES

MID TO
LATE SUMMER

Silky

Stiff

Roundleaf

Dogwoods with Blue Fruits

Cornus spp.

HABITAT: Three species of native dogwoods with blue fruits and opposite leaves inhabit our region: silky or swamp (*Cornus amomum* and its subspecies, *C. amomum* ssp. *obliqua*), stiff (*C. foemina*), and roundleaf (*C. rugosa*). They are found in mixed-wood forests, and along streams, ponds and lakes; silky and stiff dogwood also grow in low, wet areas.

GROWTH: Broad, open shrubs, typically 6 to 10 feet in height; they spread by suckering and may form colonies. Silky dogwood stems are purplish-red and finely hairy, with brown pith; branches have a smooth green base, overlaid with an open network of brown bark. Stiff dogwood has reddish twigs that turn brown with age; the pith is white. Roundleaf stems are greenish with scattered purple streaks.

LEAVES: Leaves grow oppositely, on medium-length petioles (stemlets); veins curve inward to follow the edge contour. Edges are untoothed, and often appear wavy. Silky and stiff dogwood leaves are oval with a sharp tip, 2 to 4 inches long and one-half as wide, tapering on both ends. Roundleaf dogwood leaves are broadly egg-shaped, 3 to 6 inches long and two-thirds as wide; the tip comes to a short, sharp point. Silky and stiff dogwood leaves have three to five pairs of shallow veins per side; roundleaf has six to nine pairs of slightly deeper veins.

FRUIT: Round, smooth drupes, averaging ¼ inch across, grow in flat, loose clusters at branch tips; fruit stemlets are purplish on silky and stiff dogwood, red on roundleaf. When ripe, silky and stiff dogwood fruits are medium to deep blue; roundleaf fruits are paler blue. All are inedible.

SEASON: Fruits ripen in mid to late summer.

COMPARE: Pagoda dogwood (pg. 232) has dark blue fruits on coral-red stemlets, but leaves are alternate or grow in whorls at the ends of branches. Flowering dogwood (pg. 178) has leaves that are similar to silky dogwood, but ripe fruits are red and grow in tight clusters.

NOTES: Silky dogwood is listed as endangered in Indiana.

green = key identification feature

Silky dogwood branch

Silky dogwood

Roundleaf dogwood

Roundleaf dogwood stem

LARGE
WOODY SHRUB

ALTERNATE
LEAVES

MID TO
LATE SUMMER

Highbush Blueberry

Vaccinium corymbosum

HABITAT: This native shrub is commonly cultivated, and many hybrids have been bred from it. In the wild, it is found in areas with acidic, moist soil and ample sunshine including open woods, thickets and clearings. It tolerates damp ground and is often found in boggy or swampy areas.

GROWTH: This shrub usually has several main branches and numerous side branches; it can grow to **12 feet in height**, although it is often shorter. Twigs are yellowish-green with small, **raised brown dots**; some twigs have a reddish tinge, and young stems turn red in winter. Older stems are brown, often with thin vertical furrows; the trunk has shreddy bark.

LEAVES: Alternate, oval leaves taper on both ends; edges are smooth or may have very fine teeth, and the tip is a slightly rounded point. Leaves are 1 to 2 inches long and about one-half as wide. They are deep green to bluish-green above; undersides are paler and often slightly hairy. Fall leaf color is spectacular, ranging from red to purple to orange.

FRUIT: Round berries with a **prominent five-pointed crown** on the bottom; when ripe, they are **blue with a dusty bloom**. Berries are ⅜ to ½ inch across, with **small, soft seeds**; they grow in clusters on short stemlets originating in leaf axils. Ripe berries are delicious raw or cooked. There are no toxic look-alikes with a five-pointed crown on the bottom.

SEASON: White urn-shaped flowers appear in mid to late spring. The berries that follow are green and hard at first, changing to **pink** before ripening to dusty blue in mid to late summer.

COMPARE: Upland highbush blueberry (*V. simulatum*) grows in our area in parts of eastern Ohio and Kentucky; underripe fruits are orange-red, ripe fruits purplish. Black highbush blueberry (*V. fuscatum*) is scattered in our area; ripe berries are blackish, and are smaller and less sweet than those of *V. corymbosum*. Blue Ridge and lowbush blueberries (pg. 218) have fruits and leaves that resemble highbush blueberries, but their leaves are smaller and they are short shrubs that do not exceed 3 feet in height.

NOTES: Wildlife such as birds, deer and small mammals enjoy the fruits.

green = key identification feature

Black highbush
Blueberry

LARGE
WOODY SHRUB

OPPOSITE
LEAVES

MID TO
LATE SUMMER

Withe-Rod

Viburnum nudum var. *cassinoides*

HABITAT: Openings in moist mixed-wood and coniferous forests; also found along riverbanks, in damp thickets and on swamp edges.

GROWTH: An upright native shrub with a dense, rounded crown; generally 5 to 6 feet in height but occasionally taller. Stems are brownish and slightly nubby in texture.

LEAVES: Roughly oval, tapering on both ends with a small, rounded point on the tip; 1½ to 4 inches long and one-half as wide. Edges generally have fine teeth, and may be slightly wavy; some leaves have smooth edges. Leaves grow oppositely, on **short, round petioles** (stemlets); they are smooth and firm-textured. The top surface is dark green, the underside paler; young leaves are bronze in color. Leaves turn red or purplish in fall; often, the center or base colors first, producing a splotchy appearance.

FRUIT: Oval drupes, about ⅜ inch long, grow on reddish stemlets in a flat-topped cluster (cyme); **the cluster is at the end of a stalk** that grows from the branch tip, beyond the last pair of leaves. Fruits are greenish-white when first formed, turning **hot pink** before ripening to deep blue or bluish-black with a dusty bloom. Fully ripe fruits develop a wrinkled texture, giving the plant its other common name, wild raisin. The fruits are edible, sweet and delicious. There are no toxic look-alikes.

SEASON: Fruits ripen in mid to late summer, and may persist into winter.

COMPARE: Several related shrubs with similar, edible fruits grow in our area. Blackhaw and nannyberry (pg. 296) fruits are red when underripe and black at maturity, and the fruit cluster grows directly from the last pair of leaves, with no stalk; edges of the petioles are flattened and resemble wings. Possumhaw viburnum (*V. nudum* var. *nudum*) is found in our area only in a few counties in southwestern Kentucky, where it is listed as endangered; its leaves are narrower and smooth-edged.

NOTES: The fruits have a modest amount of flesh in proportion to the pit; they make a great trail nibble, and can be pitted to use in sauces or baked goods. Withe-rod is listed as endangered in both Indiana and Kentucky.

green = key identification feature

LARGE
WOODY SHRUB

ALTERNATE
LEAVES

LATE
SUMMER

Northern Bayberry

Morella pensylvanica

HABITAT: This native plant is more common on the East coast, where it is often found on coastal sand dunes from Maine to North Carolina. In our region, it grows in open areas with sandy or loose soil. It tolerates both dry and moist conditions, and does best in sunny areas with acidic soil.

GROWTH: An upright, leafy shrub with many branches, typically 5 to 10 feet in height, bayberry spreads by suckering, often forming clumps up to 15 feet across; coastal plants are shorter. Branches are stiff and brittle; they are reddish-brown and rough-textured when young, turning brownish-gray and smooth with age. All parts of the plant are **highly fragrant**, with a pleasantly sweet, spicy scent. Bayberry is usually unisexual—a plant is either male or female, and only female plants bear fruit.

LEAVES: The smooth, glossy, thick leaves are oval to paddle-shaped, with a tapering base; they are 1½ to 4 inches long and about one-third as wide. Edges are smooth, although the tips of some leaves have several broad, shallow teeth. Leaves grow alternately on short petioles (stemlets), and also in clusters at branch tips. Leaf undersides have **small yellow resin dots** (visible with a lens) which provide fragrance to the leaves. In temperate areas, leaves remain green most of the winter.

FRUIT: Round, **bumpy, waxy, bluish-white drupes**, about ⅛ inch across, grow in tight clusters on short stalks along the stems. The fruits are inedible.

SEASON: Fruits ripen in late summer, and persist through winter.

COMPARE: Wax myrtle (*M. cerifera*) and southern bayberry (*M. caroliniensis*) are related plants with similar appearance, but their fruits are smaller, and leaves are narrower with resin glands on both surfaces; they grow in the southeastern U.S. as far west as Texas but are not found in our area.

NOTES: Some sources refer to this plant as *Myrica pensylvanica*. In Colonial days, bayberries were boiled in water to melt the wax, which was then skimmed off; wicking was dipped into the wax to make thin, fragrant candles that were traditionally burned on Christmas Eve to bring good luck. Today, some artisans still make traditional bayberry candles.

green = key identification feature

NOT EDIBLE

LARGE
WOODY SHRUB

OPPOSITE
LEAVES

LATE SUMMER
TO FALL

Southern

Smooth
*see below

Softleaf

Arrowwoods with Blue Fruits
Viburnum spp.

HABITAT: Three native arrowwoods with blue fruits are found in our area: southern (*Viburnum dentatum*), smooth (*V. recognitum*, sometimes called northern arrowwood) and softleaf (*V. molle*, also called Kentucky viburnum). They are found along streams, in moist woodlands, and on steep slopes. They grow best in moderate shade to full sun.

GROWTH: Multi-branched shrubs up to 15 feet in height; branches are **straight or gently arched.** Young stems are brownish, and are some-times velvety; they may develop slight ridges as they grow. Bark of the main trunk is gray or brown, with pale pores; it becomes **loose** on softleaf arrowwood and peels off in thin sheets.

LEAVES: Broadly egg-shaped to almost circular, with sharp, coarse teeth and deeply indented veins. Leaves grow oppositely on long petioles (stem-lets); petioles of softleaf arrowwood have **tiny reddish glands** (visible with a lens). Top sides are dark green and smooth. Undersides are paler; smooth arrowwood leaves are **smooth underneath**, while undersides of southern and softleaf are **hairy.** Leaves are typically 2 to 4½ inches long, and equally wide; smooth and softleaf have **heart-shaped bases**.

FRUIT: Smooth, rounded drupes, ¼ inch across, grow in a loose cluster **at the end of a long stalk that grows from the branch tip,** beyond the last pair of leaves. The drupes have a slight projection on the base; they are opaque blue to bluish-black when ripe. The fruits are bitter and inedible.

SEASON: Flat-topped clusters of white flowers with an unpleasant scent appear from late spring to early summer; the fruits are ripe in late sum-mer to early fall, depending on location.

COMPARE: Downy arrowwood (pg. 280) is a related plant with similar leaves, but its fruits are black when ripe. Several dogwoods in our area (pgs. 222, 232) have clusters of blue fruits, but their leaves lack the large, coarse teeth found on arrowwood.

NOTES: American Indians used the stiff, straight branches to make arrows. Softleaf is listed as threatened in Kentucky and endangered in Ohio.

green = key identification feature   *specific IN locations not available

Southern arrowwood

Peeling bark, leaf base
of softleaf arrowwood

LARGE SHRUB
OR SMALL TREE

ALTERNATE
LEAVES

MID TO
LATE SUMMER

Pagoda Dogwood

Cornus alternifolia

HABITAT: Rich, mixed-wood and deciduous forests; rocky slopes; stream and swamp borders. Prefers moderate shade and well-drained soil.

GROWTH: A large native shrub that sometimes appears as a small tree, up to 25 feet tall with a flat-topped, spreading crown. Branches are **tiered**, with upturned ends; many grow **parallel to the ground**, giving the shrub a **layered appearance**. Young stems are greenish or reddish-purple; older bark is grayish-brown, with a rough, often furrowed texture.

LEAVES: Also called alternate-leaf dogwood, pagoda is the only dogwood with **alternate leaves**, which grow sparsely along the branches. At the ends of the branches, leaves grow in **whorled clusters**. Leaves are oval, tapering on both ends, with smooth edges, a sharp tip and long petiole (stemlet). Each leaf has **five or six pairs** of distinct veins that **curve in towards the tip**; the leaf surface is somewhat pillowy between the veins. Leaves are 2 to 5 inches long and one-half as wide; they are deep green and smooth above, paler and slightly hairy below. Leaves often turn red or purplish in fall.

FRUIT: Round, dark blue drupes, ¼ inch across, grow in flat, loose clusters at branch tips. The drupes are smooth and opaque, with a slight whitish bloom; stemlets are **bright coral-red**. The fruits are inedible.

SEASON: Fruits are greenish when young, gradually becoming reddish or lavender; they ripen fully in mid to late summer.

COMPARE: Three other native dogwoods with blue fruits are found in our area, but their leaves are opposite, not alternate; please see pg. 222 for full descriptions. Some arrowwoods (pg. 230) also have blue fruits, but they have coarsely toothed leaves that grow oppositely.

NOTES: The fruits fall off or are eaten by wildlife fairly quickly, but the red stemlets remain, making an interesting display. Pagoda dogwoods are sometimes called pigeonberry because the fruits were reportedly a favorite of the now-extinct passenger pigeon (Billy Bruce Winkles; treetrail.net).

green = key identification feature

LARGE SHRUB
OR SMALL TREE

OPPOSITE
LEAVES

LATE SUMMER
TO EARLY FALL

Fringetree

Chionanthus virginicus

HABITAT: Areas with moist, well-drained soil, including woodlands, hillsides, savannas, rocky ledges and bluffs; also found along creeks and ponds. It prefers sun, but will grow in partial shade.

GROWTH: A large native shrub that sometimes appears as a small tree, fringetree can be up to 35 feet high in the wild; cultivated specimens are usually shorter. It typically has **multiple stems** at the base, and side branches are sometimes crooked, giving the shrub a **gnarly shape**. Young stems are tan or orangish, turning gray and knobby with age. The trunk is brown to gray, with rough ridges. Fringetree is unisexual—a plant is either male or female, and each produces a different type of flower. Those on the male plant are extremely showy, with an abundance of **long, thin white petals** that give the plant its other common name, old man's beard.

LEAVES: Oval leaves with a tapered base and a pointed tip are 4 to 8 inches long and one-half to one-third as wide; edges are smooth, and the mid-vein is prominent. Top sides of mature leaves are dark green and smooth, while the undersides are paler with small hairs on the veins; young leaves are yellowish-green. Leaves grow oppositely on hairy, ½-inch petioles (stemlets); at branch tips, the leaves grow so closely together that they appear **whorled**.

FRUIT: Juicy, egg-shaped drupes growing on long, thin stemlets in clusters from the branch tips on female plants. The drupes are ½ to ¾ inch long; they are green and speckled when immature, ripening to smooth **bluish-purple with a whitish bloom**. The fruits are inedible.

SEASON: Masses of white flowers appear in late spring; fruits ripen in late summer to early fall.

COMPARE: Immature fruits somewhat resemble those of Russian olive (pg. 70), but Russian olive's leaves are long and narrow with a silvery cast.

NOTES: The fleshy fruits are a valuable food for birds and other wildlife. Fringetree is listed as threatened in Ohio.

green = key identification feature

TREE

OPPOSITE
LEAVES

LATE
SUMMER

Eastern Red Cedar
Juniperus virginiana

HABITAT: Rich, moist mixed-wood forests; abandoned agricultural areas; rocky outcrops; dry hillsides and prairies; pastures and clearings. Often found in areas with limestone; occasionally found in swampy areas.

GROWTH: This columnar native evergreen tree is usually 40 to 50 feet tall when found in the wild, but can grow to 100 feet. Young twigs are greenish and scaly; branches are brownish-red. The oldest bark is shreddy, peeling off in long strips; exposed wood is gray. Eastern red cedar is generally unisexual—a plant is either male or female, and each produces a different type of fruit. It can be invasive in prairies.

LEAVES: Two types of evergreen leaves grow on eastern red cedar. The primary type are tiny scales, which overlap so tightly on small twigs that the twigs appear to be **four-sided, grayish-green scaly leaves.** Young trees and new growth have pointed, awl-like needles, which are dark blue-green and about ½ inch long, growing in whorls of three. The foliage has a strong smell which is both piney and resinous.

FRUIT: The female fruit is an oblong, berry-like cone, about ¼ inch across, that grows at the tips of scale-covered branches. Cones are **bluish, with a waxy bloom;** they are usually profuse. (Male fruits are borne on separate plants; they look like small brown, tightly lapped "pine cones" growing at the ends of branches.) Female cones reportedly can be roasted to use as a coffee substitute, but are not edible.

SEASON: Fruits ripen in late summer, and usually persist through winter.

COMPARE: Common juniper (pg. 220) is a short woody shrub with similar-looking dusty blue, rounded fruits, but its leaves are narrow, pointed, awl-like evergreen needles, similar to those on young red cedar trees. Its fruits are used as a seasoning, and are also used to flavor gin.

NOTES: Red cedar wood contains an oil that is a natural insect repellent. It is used to line chests (and make pencils), and also chipped for use as bedding for hamsters and other pet rodents.

green = key identification feature

TREE

ALTERNATE
LEAVES

LATE SUMMER
TO FALL

Sassafras

Sassafras albidum

HABITAT: This native tree is found in abandoned fields, open woodlands and forest openings, and along roads and fencerows; it often grows as a pioneer plant on disturbed sites. It produces suckers, and may form dense thickets. Sassafras grows best in sandy soil and partial shade, but will tolerate a range of soil and full sun.

GROWTH: A medium-sized tree, 30 to 60 feet in height, with a broad, rounded crown. Twigs are smooth and yellowish-green; the trunk is reddish-brown and deeply furrowed, with flat-topped ridges. Sassafras trees are unisexual—a tree is either male or female, and each produces a different type of flower.

LEAVES: Three shapes grow on sassafras trees. Some are oval, but the most characteristic leaves have **two or three lobes** with deep sinuses (the curved depression between the lobes). The lobes are not symmetrical on two-lobed leaves, so the leaf resembles a **mitten**; three-lobed leaves are fairly symmetrical. Leaves are 3 to 7 inches long and about two-thirds as wide; edges are smooth, and the base is sharply tapered. The leaves grow alternately on long, reddish petioles (stemlets); they are bright green above, and white beneath. Trees growing in alkaline soil have yellowish-green leaves with darker areas around the veins. In fall, the leaves turn yellow, orange or scarlet.

FRUIT: Oval, deep-blue drupes, about ½ inch long, grow singly or in clusters on long, **curved red stalks** at the branch tips of female trees. The top of the stalk, at the base of the fruit, is **swollen and cup-like**. The fruits are inedible.

SEASON: Fruits mature in late summer to fall.

COMPARE: Mulberries (pg. 166) have some mitten-like leaves, but the leaves are toothy and the fruits are compound drupes.

NOTES: All parts of the plant have a spicy scent, and were used medicinally by American Indians and pioneers. Ground dried leaves are sold as filé, a powder used to thicken gumbo; root bark is used to brew tea.

green = key identification feature

TREE

ALTERNATE
LEAVES

LATE SUMMER
TO FALL

Blackgum –OR– Tupelo

Nyssa sylvatica

HABITAT: This native tree thrives in areas with rich, moist soil, but also grows in dry, rocky areas. It is found next to streams and ponds, in swampy areas and creek bottoms, and in openings in damp woodlands. It prefers full sun, and is tolerant of seasonal flooding.

GROWTH: A medium to large tree, often 60 to 80 feet in height, with dense foliage and a pyramidal crown. The trunk, which may be up to 3 feet thick, is straight, and branches are horizontal or slightly drooping. Branches are smooth and gray or reddish, with small lenticels (breathing pores); the trunk is dark grayish-brown, with irregular, flat ridges.

LEAVES: Glossy, leathery oval leaves, 4 to 6 inches long and one-half as wide, grow alternately on short petioles (stemlets); leaves often cluster on short spur branches along the main branch. They are deep green on top, yellowish-green underneath. Edges are smooth, but some leaves have several very large teeth that look like pointed lobes. Leaf bases may be rounded or tapered; tips come to a blunt point. The leaves turn brilliant scarlet, orange or purplish in fall.

FRUIT: Round to oval drupes, about ½ inch long, grow singly or in small clusters on long, thin stemlets along side branches; ripe fruits are dark blue with a dusty bloom. They contain a single, large pit; the flesh is thin but juicy, with a bitter flavor reminiscent of lime peels. The fruits can be eaten in the field as an astringent refresher; according to some reports, they can also be used to make preserves.

SEASON: Fruits ripen in late summer to fall.

COMPARE: The related water tupelo (*N. aquatica*) is similar, but its trunk flares out at the base; it grows in swampy areas, and in our area is found only in western Kentucky. Persimmon (pg. 80) has similar leaves and patchy bark, but fruits are large, globe-shaped berries with a sturdy crown-like cap; its leaves are not shiny and do not turn red in fall.

NOTES: Birds devour the fruit very quickly upon its ripening. Honey made by bees feeding on tupelo flowers is very highly regarded.

green = key identification feature

TENDER
LEAFY PLANT

SINGLE
COMPOUND
LEAF

MIDSUMMER

Sarsaparilla

Aralia nudicaulis

HABITAT: Rich, moist, sun-dappled mixed-wood and hardwood forests; thickets and prairie areas; occasionally near streams and bogs.

GROWTH: This native plant has a single, three-stemmed, doubly compound leaf growing from a rhizome (an underground root-bearing stem) at the top of a long, erect, hairless leaf stalk; total height may be as much as 2 feet, but it is usually shorter. The flowering/fruiting stalk is separate, rising from the same point as the leaf stalk; it is shorter, typically 5 to 8 inches in height.

LEAVES: Three-part, doubly compound; each of the three leaf stalks has three to five oblong, toothy leaflets with rounded bases and pointed tips. Leaflets are 2 to 4 inches long and about two-thirds as wide; they are broadest at or below the midpoint.

FRUIT: The leafless fruiting stalk divides into three stemlets (occasionally two); each is topped with a rounded cluster of black berries on slender stemlets that emanate from a central point, much like the fluffy head of a dandelion gone to seed. Berries are round, and about ⅛ inch in diameter. They are inedible when raw; although they may be edible when cooked, sources disagree on this, so they are best left to the birds, foxes and bears, who consume them with no ill effects.

SEASON: Fruits ripen in midsummer.

COMPARE: Bristly sarsaparilla (*A. hispida*) has ball-shaped clusters of round, blackish berries, but the plant is much larger and leafier overall, and the lower part of the plant is very bristly. Each plant has up to 25 fruiting clusters, which rise above the leaves on long stalks. In our area, bristly sarsaparilla is found in only a few counties in northern Indiana and Ohio.

NOTES: The underground rhizome is very fragrant, and has been used to make tea and other beverages. It is not, however, the source of the flavoring in root beer and the soft drink called sarsaparilla; rather, that flavor traditionally came from the roots and bark of the unrelated sassafras tree (pg. 238).

green = key identification feature

TENDER
LEAFY PLANT

ALTERNATE
LEAVES

LATE
SUMMER

American Pokeweed

Phytolacca americana

HABITAT: Agricultural areas, waste ground, fencelines, railroad beds, field edges, shelterbelts, disturbed sites. Requires adequate moisture; can grow in sun or shade.

GROWTH: An upright, multi-branching native leafy plant, up to 12 feet in height but generally much shorter. Stems are green when young, turning reddish or purplish as they mature. The central stem often becomes quite thick, up to 1 inch in diameter.

LEAVES: Alternate, oblong leaves, up to 12 inches long and roughly one-third as wide. The base of leaf tapers into the long pink or reddish petiole (stemlet); the leaf is broadest at the midpoint, tapering to a point at the tip. Leaves are bright green and coarsely textured with smooth edges; they have an unpleasant scent when crushed.

FRUIT: The most distinctive part of the plant. Shiny, purplish-black berries with an indent in the bottom, each ¼ to ⅓ inch wide and often slightly flattened, grow in a raceme (a long cluster of multiple fruits) from hot-pink stemlets; the hanging fruit stem is also hot pink, and up to 15 inches long. The berries are poisonous, containing toxic alkaloids.

SEASON: Berries develop in early to mid summer; they are green at first, turning white with white stemlets, before ripening in late summer.

COMPARE: When it is fruiting, pokeweed is hard to miss, or to confuse with other plants. The dark berries on the hot-pink stem, combined with the overall size of the plant and its leaves, make this plant easy to identify.

NOTES: Although *all parts of the pokeweed plant contain deadly, toxic alkaloids*, young shoots of pokeweed are traditionally eaten as a cooked green, especially in the South; special preparations are needed to eliminate the toxic constituents. Sap from the plant can cause an allergic reaction in sensitive individuals. The berries can be used to produce ink and a red dye; according to some sources, the juice was used in the past to intensify the color of cheap wine.

green = key identification feature

TENDER
LEAFY PLANT

BASAL
LEAF GROWTH

LATE
SUMMER

White Clintonia –OR–
Speckled Wood Lily

Clintonia umbellulata

HABITAT: This native plant grows in colonies in moist, rich woodlands (particularly hemlock or birch forests), on wooded slopes and in ravines; it requires partial to full shade and acid soil. It is listed as threatened in Ohio.

GROWTH: Bright green leaves grow basally from a rhizome (an underground root-bearing stem). Flowers are borne on a separate leafless stalk, 8 to 18 inches in height, which grows from the center of the plant. Each stalk has a rounded cluster of 10 to 25 white flowers which are speckled with tiny purple spots; tips of the petals may be greenish.

LEAVES: Smooth, glossy, paddle-shaped leaves are up to 10 inches long and one-third as wide; the base is tapered and the tip ends in a small point. Leaves are deeply cleft by the midrib; leaf edges are smooth, with numerous fine, long hairs (visible with a lens), especially near the base. Each plant typically has two to five leaves.

FRUIT: Glossy, opaque berries grow in a rounded cluster at the end of the flowering stalk. The berry is round or a slightly flattened oval, ¼ to ⅓ inch across; it is greenish when unripe, turning deep metallic blue before ripening to black. Fruits are mildly toxic and should not be eaten.

SEASON: White clintonia flowers in late spring to early summer; the berries follow, ripening by late summer. Leaves are typically yellowed by the time the berries ripen.

COMPARE: Yellow clintonia (*C. borealis*), also called blue-bead lily, is very similar, but each plant has only three to eight flowers which are yellow, not white; ripe berries are metallic blue. Yellow clintonia is more common in cooler northern and northeastern states; in our area, it is found very occasionally in the northern parts of Indiana and Ohio.

NOTES: Leaves from young clintonia, picked just as the plants start to flower, are edible raw or cooked; they have a fresh, cucumber-like taste. By the time the plants have flowered, the leaves are tough and bitter.

green = key identification feature

Unripe berries

Ripe berries

TENDER
LEAFY PLANT

ALTERNATE
LEAVES

MIDSUMMER
TO EARLY FALL

Eastern Black Nightshade
Solanum ptycanthum

HABITAT: Agricultural areas, waste ground, urban areas, thickets, woodland openings, rocky ground and vacant lots. It does best in partial to full sun, and can adapt to moist or dry conditions.

GROWTH: A tender, branching native perennial, up to 3 feet in height but often shorter. Young stems are green and round, often with scattered hairs; they become brownish, angular and woody over the season.

LEAVES: Alternate, slightly hairy on both surfaces. Purplish when young changing to deep green, although undersides are typically tinged with purple even on mature leaves. The shape is inconsistent; in general, they are broadly triangular to elliptic, but edges may be smooth and wavy, or may have wide, blunt teeth. Larger leaves are up to 3 inches long and two-thirds as wide, although the plant typically has numerous smaller leaves near the ends of the branches.

FRUIT: Round berries, about ⅓ inch in diameter with a star-shaped cap, grow in hanging clusters of five to seven. Berries are hard and green when young, softening and ripening to a deep, glossy black; they have juicy pulp and numerous flat seeds. *Underripe berries are toxic.* Some foragers eat fully ripe berries in small quantities, but even this may cause intestinal problems in some people. For more information on judging ripeness and eating nightshade berries, consult *Nature's Garden* (Sam Thayer). To avoid potential problems, simply consider them inedible.

SEASON: Small, white, star-shaped flowers grow throughout summer; berries follow, ripening throughout midsummer and into early fall.

COMPARE: Climbing nightshade (pg. 112) grows as a vine; its fruits are red when ripe and its flowers are purple. Hoe nightshade (*S. physalifolium*) is an introduced, non-vining nightshade that is found in only a few counties in our area; ripe berries are yellowish-green, and the plant is very hairy.

NOTES: Sometimes listed as a synonym for black nightshade (*S. nigrum*); however, according to the USDA PLANTS database, *S. nigrum* is a separate species that grows on both coasts and in Canada, but not here.

green = key identification feature

WOODY
VINE

ALTERNATE
LEAVES

EARLY
SPRING

* see below

English Ivy

Hedera helix

HABITAT: English ivy was brought to the United States as an ornamental by European immigrants, and has become a noxious, invasive weed in many areas. It is found in moist, open forests, where dense mats of ivy crawl along the ground and climb trees to form large hanging clumps; it also grows in fields and disturbed areas, and tolerates dry areas and wetlands.

GROWTH: A climbing or ground-hugging woody vine, English ivy has **aerial rootlets along the stem** that secrete a sticky substance, allowing the plant to attach itself to trees, buildings, cliffs and anything else it encounters. When the vine creeps along the ground, the rootlets grow into the soil, anchoring and spreading the plant. Young stems are bumpy and greenish; older stems have grayish-brown bark. The main stems of old vines may be up to 10 inches thick.

LEAVES: Evergreen, smooth, waxy and slightly leathery; growing alternately on long petioles (stemlets) which may be tinged with red. Leaves on young plants are dark green and typically have **white veins** or, sometimes, **white edges**; they are 2 to 4 inches in length and width, and have three to five lobes, each ending in a softly rounded point. Mature, flowering stems have unlobed leaves that are often lighter in color.

FRUIT: Rounded bluish-black drupes, about ¼ inch across with several bumps and wrinkles on the base, grow in clusters on long stemlets on older vines. The fruits are mildly toxic and should not be eaten.

SEASON: English ivy does not flower or produce fruits until it is as much as 10 years old. In late summer, clusters of greenish-yellow flowers appear on mature plants that receive adequate sunlight, followed by fruits which remain green until ripening the following spring.

COMPARE: Leaves and fruits resemble wild grapes (pgs. 190, 192, 254), but unlike grapes, English ivy has no tendrils; more importantly, English ivy fruits ripen in early spring and are long gone by the time grapes appear.

NOTES: English ivy can smother and kill the trees it climbs on; the added foliage also makes the trees more vulnerable to windstorms.

green = key identification feature   *specific IN locations not available

Aerial rootlets

Ripe fruit

TENDER OR
WOODY VINE

ALTERNATE
LEAVES

MID TO
LATE SUMMER

* see below

Smilax

Smilax spp.

HABITAT: These native vines grow in openings in moist, rich deciduous forests; also streambanks, thickets, clearings and waste ground.

GROWTH: *Smilax* is a family of vines, up to 10 feet in length. Some use tendrils to climb over other plants, while others lack tendrils, reclining over other plants when they become too tall to support themselves. There are two types of *Smilax*: non-woody (also called carrion-flower) and woody (also called greenbrier). In our area, non-woody species include common *Smilax* (*Smilax lasioneura*), upright (*S. ecirrhata*), smooth (*S. herbacea*), Illinois (*S. illinoensis*), Huger's (*S. hugeri*) and downy (*S. pulverulenta*). Woody species include catbrier (*S. rotundifolia*), bristly greenbrier (*S. tamnoides*), whiteleaf greenbrier (*S. glauca*) and saw greenbrier (*S. bona-nox*). Woody species have bristles and, sometimes, thorns.

LEAVES: Most *Smilax* in our area have broadly oval or heart-shaped leaves, with several **deep parallel veins that have a web of smaller veins** between them. Saw greenbrier leaves, however, have **three rounded** lobes that lack the web of veins; leaf edges are spiny. Leaves of all *Smilax* grow alternately along the stem; they are generally 3 to 5 inches long and one-half to three-quarters as wide. Most are dark green on top, paler underneath; whiteleaf greenbrier are **white underneath**, and saw greenbrier may have **light splotches** on top.

FRUIT: Both woody and non-woody *Smilax* produce similar **rounded or ball-shaped clusters of berries on long, stiff stalks**. Ripe fruits of all *Smilax* in our area are bluish-black with a whitish bloom. The fruits are generally considered edible but are rubbery and distasteful; they are not eaten.

SEASON: Berries ripen in mid to late summer, and may persist into winter.

COMPARE: The berry cluster may be mistaken for wild grapes (pgs. 190, 192, 254); however, the stalk on *Smilax* makes identification easy.

NOTES: For information that helps identify many of the *Smilax* in our area, please visit the website of the Robert W. Freckmann Herbarium (University of Wisconsin, Stevens Point) at http://wisplants.uwsp.edu.

green = key identification feature   *combined range

Common carrion-flower

Lower stem of
bristly greenbrier

WOODY
VINE

ALTERNATE
LEAVES

LATE SUMMER
TO FALL

Frost

Graybark

Catbird

Black Wild Grapes

Vitis spp.

HABITAT: Three native wild grapes with blackish fruits are locally common in our area: frost or winter grape (*Vitis vulpina*), graybark grape (*V. cinerea*) and catbird or red grape (*V. palmata*). All are found in moist, rich, sunny areas including thickets, streambanks and woodland margins; catbird grapes tolerate very wet areas and often grow in sloughs or swamps.

GROWTH: Woody, high-climbing vines, up to 60 feet long, with shreddy bark on the trunk; they use **forked tendrils** to climb. Catbird stems are **red**; the others are green or brown, and those of graybark are **angular**.

LEAVES: Heart-shaped leaves grow alternately on long petioles (stemlets). Frost and catbird have sharp teeth on the edges; graybark has **shallow teeth** which may be rounded. Catbird leaves are 3 to 5 inches long and have **three distinct lobes with long, pointed tips and deep, rounded depressions between the lobes.** Graybark and frost grape leaves are up to 6 inches long and are unlobed or with shallow lobes. Leaves of graybark grapes are **whitish below**; the others are greenish.

FRUIT: Loose clusters of edible round, juicy berries, each ¼ to ⅜ inch across, hang from the vine on stalks opposite a leaf; each grape has one to four **teardrop-shaped seeds.** Frost grapes are **blackish with a waxy bloom**; graybark's are similar but have **no bloom.** Both are acidic, turning sweeter after a frost. Catbird grapes are **bluish-black with little or no bloom**; they have thick skins and large seeds but the pulp is sweet.

SEASON: Catbird grapes are ripe in late summer through early fall; frost and graybark grapes are ripe from early through mid fall.

COMPARE: Several species of grapes in our area have edible purplish fruits (pgs. 190, 192). Wild grapes may be confused with several inedible or toxic fruits; please see "Be certain, be safe: Wild grapes" on pg. 20.

NOTES: Common names used for grapes are confusing. *V. vulpina* is often called fox grape, a name which is more commonly used for *V. labrusca* (pg. 190); *V. cinerea* is sometimes called winter grape, which is one of the common names used here for *V. vulpina*.

green = key identification feature

Frost grape

Ripe
frost grapes

Catbird grape leaves

Graybark grape leaves, stem

WOODY
VINE

ALTERNATE
COMPOUND
LEAVES

LATE SUMMER
TO FALL

* see below

Pepppervine

Ampelopsis arborea

HABITAT: Wet areas, including marshes, floodplains, and swamps; along streams and rivers; in abandoned fields, road ditches and low thickets. It produces abundant fruit in full sun, less in shady areas.

GROWTH: This native vine often sprawls along the ground like a ground-cover, but is more often a high-climbing vine. It can grow to 35 feet in length; it is typically a very full, **bushy** plant, whether reclining or climbing. Young stems are **reddish** and often have fine hairs; older stems are brownish and woody, with warty lenticels (breathing pores). It has **occasional tendrils** opposite the leaves.

LEAVES: **Twice- or thrice-divided compound leaves** grow alternately. Each leaf is 3 to 7 inches long and almost as wide; the leaf stalk is **reddish**, and **grooved on one side**. Two to six compound leaflets grow from each leaf stalk; a terminal three-part compound leaflet is also present. Individual leaflets are up to 1½ inches long and about two-thirds as wide, with very coarse teeth; they are dark green and smooth above, lighter green below with scattered hairs on the veins. Young leaves are reddish and very shiny. The foliage turns yellowish or red in fall.

FRUIT: Round or slightly flattened berries, ¼ to ⅜ inch across, grow in loose clusters on leafless stemlets. Berries are pale when young, turning bright red before ripening to shiny black. Some sources list the fruit as edible, but most reliable sources say that edibility is questionable and the flavor poor. It is best to treat them as inedible.

SEASON: Berries are ripe from late summer to fall.

COMPARE: Fruits may resemble grapes (pgs. 190, 192, 254), but grapes do not have compound leaves. The leaves are similar to those of trumpet creeper (*Campsis radicans*), a native vine found throughout much of our area; however, trumpet creeper's fruits are long pods.

NOTES: Pepppervine grows vigorously and spreads aggressively, and is considered a nuisance plant in some areas. Small mammals eat the fruits; deer occasionally browse on the leaves.

green = key identification feature   *specific IN locations not available

WOODY VINE

ALTERNATE LEAVES

LATE SUMMER TO FALL

Cupseed

Calycocarpum lyonii

HABITAT: Areas with rich, moist soil including streambanks, floodplain forests, river bottoms, valleys and field edges.

GROWTH: A native woody vine, up to 30 feet in length, that climbs by twining itself around fences, trees and other plants; it has no tendrils. It may die back to the ground in winter; new growth is tender and green, so the vine may appear non-woody. Stems are smooth and yellowish-brown to gray, with fine grooves and dark speckles.

LEAVES: Alternate, on petioles (stemlets) that are up to 6 inches long. Leaves are generally palmately lobed, but some are heart-shaped (unlobed). The lobed leaves, 3 to 8 inches long and almost as wide, have three to five lobes with pointed tips; the sinuses (depressions between the lobes) are deep around the central lobe, shallower between the other lobes (when present). Unlobed leaves are typically 3 to 6 inches long and almost as wide; they are broadest at the base, and may have scattered large teeth. The upper sides of all leaves are smooth and bright green; undersides are slightly paler, with scattered hairs on the veins.

FRUIT: Thin-fleshed round or oval drupes grow in tight, hanging clusters on a long, thin stalk opposite a leaf. The fruits are ¾ to 1 inch long, and black or yellowish-black when ripe, with no bloom; each contains a single, very large seed shaped like a rounded cup. The fruits are inedible.

SEASON: Fruits are ripe in late summer to fall.

COMPARE: Cupseed's fruit clusters are 2 to 3 inches long and bear a resemblance to grapes (pgs. 190, 192, 254); also, cupseed's leaves are similar to some grape species. Grapes have tendrils, which are absent on cupseed; grape seeds are small and egg-shaped. Care is needed when picking grapes in areas where cupseed is also present.

NOTES: Cupseed is a member of the moonseed (pg. 194) family. The first part of its botanical name, *Calycocarpum*, comes from the Greek words for "cup" and "fruit" (*calyx* and *carpos*), chosen for the cup-like shape of the seed. Cupseed is listed as threatened in Indiana.

green = key identification feature

258

Unripe fruit

Cup-shaped seed, thin flesh of fruit

WOODY
VINE

OPPOSITE
LEAVES

LATE SUMMER
TO FALL

Japanese Honeysuckle

Lonicera japonica

HABITAT: This non-native vine has escaped from cultivation, and is increasingly found in a wide variety of habitats including agricultural areas, thickets, woodlands, disturbed areas and alongside roads and railroads. It tolerates shade, but also grows in sunny areas.

GROWTH: A trailing or climbing vine, typically less than 10 feet in length but sometimes longer; it grows compactly and so profusely that it often resembles a shrub from a distance. It has **no tendrils**, and climbs by twining itself around poles, fences, trees and other plants; it can girdle and kill trees with its twining stems. It often forms **dense canopies** in forested areas. Young stems are reddish-brown and hairy; older stems and the trunk are tan, with **shreddy bark**.

LEAVES: Oval leaves, 1 to 3 inches long and one-half to two-thirds as wide, grow oppositely on short petioles (stemlets). Leaf bases are broad; the tip is often pointed, but may also be rounded. Top sides are bright green, often with fine hairs but sometimes almost smooth; undersides are paler, with hairs along the main vein. **Leaves remain green and on the plant** until the temperatures drop well below freezing; in protected areas, they may remain through winter.

FRUIT: Round to oval berries, about ¼ inch long, grow **singly or in pairs on stubby stalks** from leaf axils. Berries are juicy, and contain two or more small seeds; they are glossy black when ripe. They are inedible.

SEASON: Fragrant whitish flowers are present in late spring, turning yellow with age. Berries follow, ripening to black in late summer to fall.

COMPARE: Several native honeysuckle vines grow in our area, but ripe fruits are red, and the leaves at the tip of the stem fuse to form a cup; please see pg. 114 for more information.

NOTES: Japanese honeysuckle is native to Asia; it was brought to this country in the early 1800s as an ornamental and for erosion control. It is considered a noxious, invasive plant due to its rapid, dense growth, which often shades out native plants.

green = key identification feature

SMALL
WOODY SHRUB

ALTERNATE
COMPOUND
LEAVES

EARLY TO
MID SUMMER

Black Raspberry

Rubus occidentalis

HABITAT: Disturbed areas, especially those that have been logged or cut. Also found in tangled meadows, along streams and lakes, next to trails or roads, and in open woods. This native plant grows in both shady and sunny areas, but produces more fruit in moderate to full sun.

GROWTH: Black raspberries are brambles, sprawling vine-like shrubs that often form a thicket. Stems, called canes, grow to 6 feet in length, and usually arch but may also be upright. Black raspberry canes are round and have sharp, curved thorns. Young canes are unbranched and have a whitish bloom; older canes are branched and purplish.

LEAVES: The compound leaves grow alternately on long, smooth petioles (stemlets). Leaves usually have three leaflets, occasionally five. The terminal leaflet has a long stemlet; side leaflets attach directly to the stem. Leaflets have doubly toothed edges, with a sharply pointed tip and a rounded base; they are up to 3 inches long, and whitish below.

FRUIT: A compound drupe, up to ½ inch across. Fruits are green and hard at first, progressing through several color changes and becoming yellowish, salmon-colored, bright red, purplish-red, and finally ripening to purplish-black. Ripe fruits detach cleanly from the plant, leaving the receptacle (core) behind; the picked fruit is hollow. Fruits are edible and delicious. When the fruits are ripe, there are no toxic look-alikes.

SEASON: Black raspberries ripen in early to mid summer, generally before red raspberries (pg. 124) and well before blackberries (pg. 272).

COMPARE: Red raspberries (pg. 124) look like underripe black raspberries; however, red raspberry canes are prickly but not thorny and lack the whitish bloom. If you find raspberries that are red but hard and won't detach from the receptacle (core), you've found underripe black raspberries. Blackberries (pg. 272) have similar growth habits and a black compound fruit, but stems are ridged and have no bloom; picked fruit is not hollow.

NOTES: Many foragers consider black raspberries to be the tastiest in the *Rubus* family (which includes blackberries, dewberries and raspberries).

green = key identification feature

SMALL WOODY SHRUB

 ALTERNATE COMPOUND LEAVES

 MIDSUMMER

 Smooth

 Swamp

Black Dewberries

Rubus spp.

HABITAT: Ten varieties of native black dewberries may be found in our region; the two listed here are the most common. Smooth or common dewberry (*Rubus flagellaris*) is found in dry, open forests, fields and thickets, and along streambanks. Swamp or bristly dewberry (*R. hispidus*) prefers areas with more moisture such as bogs and low woods.

GROWTH: Dewberries are trailing, low-growing shrubs that may appear vine-like. Stems are woody but weak, usually sprawling along the ground rather than rising erect; the tips often develop roots. Smooth dewberry stems have scattered curved prickles but are not bristly. Swamp dewberry stems are well covered with fine bristles but have no prickles.

LEAVES: The compound leaves grow alternately on long petioles (stemlets) that are usually hairy or prickly. Leaves of fruiting stems have three leaflets, while those of non-fruiting stems typically have five. Leaflets are up to 3 inches long and one-half to two-thirds as wide; edges have sharp teeth.

FRUIT: The compound drupe, ¼ to ½ inch across, resembles a small blackberry; unlike blackberries, the ripe fruit detaches cleanly (but not easily) from the receptacle (core) so it is hollow when picked. Dewberry fruits are green at first, turning red before ripening to glossy black or purplish-black. All are edible; there are no toxic look-alikes with black fruits. Most are delicious, but quality varies between species and even from plant to plant. When picking, taste a few before harvesting in quantity.

SEASON: Dewberries in our area ripen in midsummer.

COMPARE: Blackberries (pg. 272) have similar fruits which are black when ripe, but they are an arching or upright shrub; they do not root at the tips. Dwarf red raspberry (pg. 124) is a dewberry that is red when ripe.

NOTES: It's easy to tell when you've found a dewberry, but often difficult to identify the exact species. Some varieties grow in only a few counties per state, but may be locally common in those areas. Because all dewberries are edible, exact identification is not critical; it is a matter for experts.

green = key identification feature

SMALL
WOODY SHRUB

ALTERNATE
LEAVES

MID TO
LATE SUMMER

Missouri Gooseberry
Ribes missouriense

HABITAT: Open woodlands, field borders, clearings, meadows, thickets, and abandoned fields.

GROWTH: An arching native shrub up to 4 feet high. Mature stems typically have scattered thin bristles; smaller stems are usually smooth. Leaf nodes have one to three long thorns that are up to ½ inch long.

LEAVES: Attached alternately to the stem by a long petiole (stemlet); each leaf node has one to three leaves. Each leaf has three to five distinct lobes, resembling a maple leaf with rounded teeth. Leaves are slightly hairy underneath.

FRUIT: The smooth, ¼- to ½-inch round berry grows on a thin stemlet from leaf nodes, singly or in clusters of two or three. Distinct stripes run longitudinally on the berry; a prominent flower remnant, often called a pigtail, is present at the end of the berry. Missouri gooseberries are green when young, maturing to deep purplish-black when ripe. Gooseberries are edible in both the green and ripe stages.

SEASON: Ripe fruits are present from midsummer in the southern part of our region, into late summer in the northern part.

COMPARE: Three other native gooseberries inhabit our region. Stems of prickly gooseberry (pg. 198) have scattered small bristles; ripe fruits are reddish-purple and bear small, soft prickles. Stems of smooth gooseberry (pg. 198) are smooth or slightly hairy; ripe fruits are purple or purplish-black, with smooth skins. Stems of Appalachian gooseberry (*R. rotundifolium*; in our area, found only in scattered locations in Ohio and Kentucky) are smooth or slightly hairy; ripe fruits are black and are dotted with yellow resin glands, which are also present on the leaf undersides. Currant shrubs (pgs. 128, 268) resemble gooseberry shrubs, but the berries are typically borne in racemes (long clusters of multiple fruits).

NOTES: Ripe gooseberries are excellent in baked desserts, sauces and other dishes. Green gooseberries (pg. 48) are rich in pectin, and are used for jam and jelly. Missouri gooseberry is listed as endangered in Ohio.

green = key identification feature

Large thorns

SMALL
WOODY SHRUB

ALTERNATE
LEAVES

MID TO
LATE SUMMER

American
*see below

Golden
*see below

Black Currants

Ribes spp.

HABITAT: Two varieties of native black currant inhabit our region: American black currant (*Ribes americanum*) and golden currant (*R. aureum*, sometimes listed as *R. odoratum*). They inhabit moist woodlands, swampy areas, thickets and streambanks; golden currant prefers rocky areas.

GROWTH: A straggling shrub, generally 3 to 6 feet in height, that often clambers over other plants; golden currant can reach 9 feet in height. Both currants listed here have smooth stems and are thornless.

LEAVES: Attached alternately to the stem by a thin petiole (stemlet). Each leaf has three to five distinct lobes, resembling a small, roughly textured maple leaf. Leaves of American black currant are rough in texture and have tiny resin dots on both surfaces (visible with a lens); those of golden currant are smooth, with no resin dots. Leaves of American black currant have pointed teeth around the entire edge except the base; golden currant leaves have a few rounded teeth at the ends of the lobes.

FRUIT: Round ¼- to ⅜-inch berries grow in a raceme (a long cluster of multiple fruits). Immature berries are green, turning red before ripening to black; a prominent flower remnant, often called a pigtail, is present at the end of the berry. Although they are a bit seedy, the currants listed here are delicious and can be eaten raw, used in baking, or cooked into jelly, jam and other dishes. There are no toxic look-alikes.

SEASON: Black currants ripen in mid to late summer.

COMPARE: Red currants (pg. 128) are similar, but berries are red when ripe. Gooseberries (pgs. 48, 198, 266) have similar leaves and growth habits, but gooseberries have thorns at the leaf nodes. Gooseberry fruits grow in clusters of two or three, in contrast to currants, which grow in a raceme.

NOTES: Golden currant, also called clove currant or buffalo currant, has a clove-like odor. Currants have been deliberately eradicated in many areas because they are an alternate host for white pine blister rust, a disease that kills white pine trees.

green = key identification feature   *specific KY, IN locations not available

American black currant

Golden currant

SMALL
WOODY SHRUB

ALTERNATE
LEAVES

MID TO
LATE SUMMER

Black Huckleberry

Gaylussacia baccata

HABITAT: Dry habitat, including rocky or sandy areas, open mixed-wood forests, thickets; fairly common in mountainous or hilly areas.

GROWTH: An upright, multi-stemmed native shrub, up to 3 feet in height but usually shorter; often grows in colonies. Branches are greenish or reddish; older stems are gray.

LEAVES: Alternate, roughly oval, tapering at both ends; dark green on top, slightly lighter beneath, with tiny golden resin dots on both surfaces (visible with a lens). Small reddish-purple spots are often present. Leaves are 1 to 3 inches long and one-third to one-half as wide; edges are smooth. They grow on a short petiole (stemlet).

FRUIT: The round berry has a small but noticeable five-pointed crown on the bottom; when ripe, fruit is black to blackish-blue with a slight bloom. Berries are typically ¼ to ½ inch across, and have greenish flesh with 10 small seeds that are soft but usually noticeable. They grow in small clusters or short racemes (clusters of multiple fruits) originating along the stem. Ripe huckleberries are usually delicious raw or cooked, although quality varies from plant to plant. There are no toxic look-alikes.

SEASON: Berries ripen in mid to late summer.

COMPARE: Huckleberries may be mistaken for Blue Ridge blueberries (pg. 218); however, ripe blueberries are bright blue with a whitish bloom, and their leaves lack the resin dots found on huckleberry leaves. Blueberries are edible and delicious; their seeds are smaller and softer than those of the huckleberry. Box huckleberry (*G. brachycera*) is a rare plant, found in our area only in southeastern Kentucky; it has twigs with angular edges and leathery, shiny evergreen leaves that rarely exceed 1 inch in length. Its fruits are blue with a pronounced bloom; they are edible but tasteless.

NOTES: Huckleberries and blueberries often grow in the same places. Distinguishing between the two is more a matter of curiosity than of necessity, because they can be used in exactly the same manner as one another.

green = key identification feature

Unripe berries

SMALL
WOODY SHRUB

ALTERNATE
COMPOUND
LEAVES

MID TO
LATE SUMMER

Blackberries

Rubus allegheniensis and others

HABITAT: Scrubby areas, waste ground, pastures, sun-dappled woods, forest clearings and thickets; also found alongside paths and roads.

GROWTH: Blackberries are brambles, sprawling vine-like shrubs that may form a thicket. Stems, called canes, grow to 8 feet in length, and are usually arching but may be upright. Blackberry canes are ridged, and star-shaped in cross-section, with numerous sharp thorns that are often curved. Young canes are reddish or greenish, with no whitish bloom; older canes are brownish. More than a dozen blackberry varieties grow in our area; several are introduced, but most are native. Some have fewer thorns; they may have smaller leaves or longer fruit clusters, and the depth of the teeth on the leaves varies. All produce edible fruit; exact identification is a matter for botanists.

LEAVES: Compound, doubly toothy, coarsely textured leaves with sharply pointed tips and long stems are attached alternately to the canes; undersides are pale. Leaves of fruiting canes have three leaflets, while those of non-fruiting canes typically have five. Leaflets are up to 5 inches long; the terminal leaflet is often larger than side leaflets.

FRUIT: A compound drupe, about ½ inch across and usually somewhat longer. Fruits are green and hard at first, turning red before ripening to glossy black. The receptacle (core) remains inside the picked berry so the fruit is solid, not hollow like a raspberry. Blackberries are edible raw or cooked; there are no toxic look-alikes in our area with black fruits.

SEASON: Blackberries are red and underripe in early summer; they ripen in mid to late summer, well after red raspberries (pg. 124) and black raspberries (pg. 262).

COMPARE: Several other *Rubus* in our area have black compound drupes. Black raspberries (pg. 262) are hollow when picked; stems are round, with a whitish bloom on young growth. Dewberries (pgs. 124, 264) are trailing rather than arching or upright shrubs; picked fruits are hollow.

NOTES: Blackberries have larger, coarser seeds than other brambles.

green = key identification feature

SMALL
WOODY SHRUB

ALTERNATE
LEAVES

LATE SUMMER
TO EARLY FALL

* see below

Alder-Leaved Buckthorn

Rhamnus alnifolia

HABITAT: Moist areas, including mixed-wood forests, damp meadows, swampy areas, streambanks and thickets. Sometimes found growing on the wet edge of a pond or lake.

GROWTH: A short, upright shrub, 3 feet or less in height with equal spread. Branches fork several times. Twigs are smooth and reddish or brownish; young branches are downy. It may form colonies, with many short shrubs in a tight group. Alder-leaved buckthorn is usually unisexual—a plant is either male or female, and each produces a different type of flower.

LEAVES: Roughly oval, with a sharp tip; each has six to eight pairs of deep, gently curving veins. Leaves are up to 4 inches long and one-half as wide; they grow alternately from the stems on short, smooth petioles (stemlets). Edges are finely toothed; both surfaces are smooth and somewhat glossy, although the veins may be slightly hairy on the underside. Tiny paired, leaf-like appendages called stipules grow at the base of each leaf petiole where it joins the main stem.

FRUIT: Glossy round drupes, about ¼ inch in diameter, are red when underripe, turning black when ripe. Fruits grow on thin stemlets from the leaf axils. They are inedible.

SEASON: Fruits are red in late summer, turning black by early fall.

COMPARE: Lanceleaf buckthorn (pg. 278) is much taller, and is found in drier habitat; its leaves are longer, and are generally narrower in proportion to their length than those of alder-leaved buckthorn. Common buckthorn (pg. 282) is another taller shrub found in drier habitat; its leaves are more egg-shaped. Glossy buckthorn (pg. 294) is also taller; it has smooth-edged leaves, and leaf undersides are hairy.

NOTES: Unlike common buckthorn and glossy buckthorn, alder-leaved buckthorn is a native plant; it is not considered invasive, and can sometimes be hard to find. It is a favored late-summer food of black bears.

green = key identification feature   *specific KY locations not available

LARGE
WOODY SHRUB

ALTERNATE
LEAVES

MID TO
LATE SUMMER

* see below

Sand Cherry

Prunus pumila

HABITAT: Open dunes; sandy or gravelly shorelines of lakes and rivers; sandy or rocky edges of coniferous forests; grassy prairie areas. Sand cherry prefers sunny areas and tolerates dry conditions; it can survive harsh winters.

GROWTH: A sparse, low native shrub, 2 to 9 feet in height, with upright branches. In windy areas, it may recline rather than stand upright. Twigs are reddish; branches are reddish-brown, becoming gray with age. Bark is marked with light-colored lenticels (breathing pores).

LEAVES: Narrowly oval, tapering on both ends, with a leathery texture; they grow alternately from the stems on petioles (stemlets) that are often reddish. Leaves are 1 to 2 inches long and roughly one-third as wide; edges have scattered small teeth, especially toward the tip. Deep green and glossy on top, lighter beneath; tips and leaf edges sometimes have a reddish tinge.

FRUIT: An oval drupe with a single pit; the fruit is about 1 inch long and glossy black when ripe. There is more flesh in proportion to the pit than on chokecherries (pg. 148) or pin cherries (pg. 172). Fruits are edible; they are sweet but somewhat astringent. They are usually cooked to make jam or preserves. There are no toxic look-alikes.

SEASON: Fruits ripen from mid to late summer.

COMPARE: Sesquehana sand cherry (*P. susquehanae*) is a related small shrub with similar leaves and fruits which is found in our area only rarely in Indiana and Ohio; its twigs are hairy and it prefers acidic soil.

NOTES: The deep roots of sand cherry help stabilize sand dunes around the Great Lakes. The fruit is eaten by large birds; twigs are browsed by deer and small mammals. Birds use the shrubs for nesting and escape cover. Sand cherry leaves, stems and pits contain hydrocyanic acid, a cyanide-producing compound. The leaves and pits should never be eaten, and care should be taken to avoid crushing the pits when juicing the fruits. Cooking or drying eliminates the harmful compounds.

green = key identification feature   *specific KY locations not available

LARGE
WOODY SHRUB

ALTERNATE
LEAVES

LATE
SUMMER

Lanceleaf Buckthorn

Rhamnus lanceolata

HABITAT: This native shrub is found in areas with a limestone base, including brushy thickets and open, wooded slopes. It prefers moist areas, and may be found near bogs and swamps, but it also tolerates drier soil. It does best in areas with partial shade.

GROWTH: Generally a medium to large shrub, up to 12 feet in height, although it can be much shorter in some locations, remaining under 6 feet. Twigs are slender and greenish to reddish with fine hairs; branches are gray. The trunk is smooth and gray, with horizontal lenticels (breathing pores); bark of older specimens may peel off in vertical strips.

LEAVES: Oval to almost lance-shaped leaves are up to 4 inches long and one-third as wide; the tip is softly pointed and the leaf base is tapered. Edges are finely toothed, and may appear slightly wavy; the top surface is deep green and smooth, while the underside is yellowish-green with scattered hairs on the midrib. Leaves grow alternately on ½-inch petioles (stemlets) that are slightly grooved and have fine hairs along the edge; leaves tend to bunch slightly at the branch tips, appearing almost opposite.

FRUIT: Round drupes, about ¼ inch across, grow in clusters on thin stemlets originating in the leaf axils. Fruits are green at first, turning dull red before ripening to black. The fruits are inedible.

SEASON: Greenish-yellow flowers appear in late spring to early summer; fruits follow, and are ripe in late summer.

COMPARE: Carolina buckthorn (pg. 162) has a very similar appearance, but it is generally taller; its leaves are a bit narrower and its fruits remain red until late fall. Alder-leaved buckthorn (pg. 274) is a related native shrub that is much shorter, usually 3 feet or less, with leaves that are up to 4 inches long. Common buckthorn (pg. 282) is a large shrub with black fruits and similar growth habit, but its leaves are wide and egg-shaped.

NOTES: Lanceleaf buckthorn provides food and shelter for wild birds.

green = key identification feature

LARGE
WOODY SHRUB

*OPPOSITE
LEAVES

LATE
SUMMER

Downy Arrowwood

Viburnum rafinesquianum

HABITAT: Dry mixed-wood and hardwood forests; wooded slopes; along streams. Downy arrowwood is drought-tolerant, and very adaptable.

GROWTH: An open, multi-branched native shrub with a rounded top, generally 6 to 8 feet in height and slightly less wide. Branches are erect and straight, spreading outward from the base. The bark is smooth and dark gray; unlike other *Viburnums*, the bark does not become flaky with age.

LEAVES: Opposite, dark green leaves with 10 or fewer pairs of large teeth grow on short, hairy, grooved petioles (stemlets); leaves are 1½ to 3 inches long and roughly one-third as wide. Leaves are broadest below the midpoint, with a rounded base; they taper to the pointed tip. Leaf edges have very fine hairs (visible with a lens); undersides are densely hairy (particularly on the veins) and light green. Foliage turns rosy maroon in the fall.

FRUIT: Oval to round drupes, about ⅓ inch long, grow in flat-topped clusters (cymes) on a stalk that grows from the branch tip, beyond the last pair of leaves; fruit stemlets are yellowish to reddish. Fruits are greenish, turning blue, then ripening to shiny bluish-black. The fruits are very bitter, with thin flesh in proportion to the pits, and are generally regarded as inedible.

SEASON: Downy arrowwood produces flat-topped clusters (cymes) of showy white flowers, which smell unpleasant, in early summer. Fruits ripen in late summer.

COMPARE: Blackhaw and nannyberry (pg. 296) produce clusters of black fruit, but the leaves have fine teeth; blackhaw and nannyberry fruits are larger, and grow directly from the leaf cluster with no central stalk. Several arrowwoods in our area have blue fruits; please see pg. 230.

NOTES: Arrowwood was used to make arrows, because the branches are long and straight. Fruits of downy arrowwood were reportedly eaten by American Indian peoples in Canada (*Traditional Plant Foods of Canadian Indigenous Peoples,* Harriet V. Kuhnlein and Nancy J. Turner). Sometimes spelled *V. rafinesqueanum*; listed as threatened in Kentucky.

green = key identification feature

LARGE
WOODY SHRUB

OPPOSITE
LEAVES

LATE SUMMER
TO EARLY FALL

Common Buckthorn
Rhamnus cathartica

HABITAT: Open hardwood forests, prairie areas, fields, forest edges, urban parks, shelterbelts, floodplains, ravines and fencerows. Prefers partial shade but can tolerate moist or dry conditions.

GROWTH: A large, multi-stemmed shrub with a spreading crown, sometimes appearing to be a small tree; up to 20 feet in height but usually much shorter. Bark is gray to brown; older stems are roughly textured, with long, corky protrusions. Twigs often have a spine at the tip, giving the species its common name.

LEAVES: Dark, glossy green, broadly oval, with a pointed tip and a broad base; leaves grow oppositely on long petioles (stemlets). Leaves are 1½ to 3 inches long, and roughly two-thirds as wide; both surfaces are hairless. Edges are finely toothy; each leaf has three to five pairs of deep veins that curve in toward the tip to follow the edge of the leaf. Leaves remain green late into fall, long after most other shrubs have lost their leaves.

FRUIT: Glossy, round black drupes, about ¼ inch in diameter, grow on thin stemlets in dense clusters at leaf axils, or singly along the stems. The fruits are strongly cathartic, and are considered toxic.

SEASON: Common buckthorn ripens in late summer to early fall.

COMPARE: Lanceleaf buckthorn (pg. 278) has very narrow leaves that are one-third as wide as they are long. Glossy buckthorn (pg. 294) has smooth-edged leaves that are typically alternate; leaf undersides are hairy, and the twigs lack the spine at the tip. Some dogwoods (pgs. 222, 232, 310) have leaves with similar curving veins, but the fruits are blue or white and borne in umbrella-shaped clusters.

NOTES: Common buckthorn is a non-native species, imported in the late 1800s from Europe for use as a landscape plant. It has naturalized, and is considered invasive throughout most of its range. It spreads rapidly, crowding out native plants.

green = key identification feature

LARGE
WOODY SHRUB

OPPOSITE
LEAVES

LATE SUMMER
TO EARLY FALL

* see below

European Privet –AND–
Border Privet

Ligustrum spp.

HABITAT: Privets are non-native shrubs that have escaped into the wild, especially near urban areas where they are planted as ornamentals. Two of the more common species in our area are European privet (*Ligustrum vulgare*) and border privet (*L. obtusifolium*). They can be found in thickets, disturbed areas and bottomland forests, as well as along roadsides and forest edges. They prefer sun, but tolerate shade in areas of rich soil.

GROWTH: Privets are leafy, multi-branched shrubs that may grow to 15 feet in height and width; they spread by suckering and often form dense thickets. Branches are brownish-gray, with numerous lenticels (breathing pores); they tend to be long and arching. The trunk is often hard to see due to all the leaves; it is gray and rough but not fissured.

LEAVES: Glossy, oval to lance-shaped leaves that taper on both ends grow oppositely on short, hairy petioles (stemlets); leaf edges are untoothed. Leaves often grow at almost a right angle to the branch. Leaf shape is variable among the privets. Those of European privet are typically narrower, up to 2½ inches long and one-quarter as wide; border privet's leaves are typically a bit shorter and one-half as wide, with a rounded tip. Border privet leaves are hairy underneath, particularly on the midvein; undersides are hairless on European privet.

FRUIT: Oval to round drupes, ¼ to ⅓ inch long, grow in large clusters at branch tips; they also are scattered in smaller clusters along the branches. Ripe fruits are glossy black to purplish-black. The fruits are considered toxic, reportedly causing intestinal problems.

SEASON: Fruits ripen from late summer to early fall, and may persist through winter; leaves may remain green through winter.

COMPARE: Lanceleaf buckthorn (pg. 278) and other buckthorns have black berries, but leaf edges are toothy and the plants aren't as full as privet.

NOTES: Considered an invasive species due to its aggressive growth.

green = key identification feature   *combined range; specific IN locations not available

Border privet (unripe)

European privet

LARGE
WOODY SHRUB

OPPOSITE
LEAVES

LATE SUMMER
TO EARLY FALL

Mapleleaf Viburnum

Viburnum acerifolium

HABITAT: This native shrub, also called dockmackie, is a common under-story plant in open woodlands, particularly beech-maple forests; it also grows on hillsides and alongside ravines. It prefers dappled shade and moist, well-drained soil, but grows well in deep shade and dry conditions.

GROWTH: A somewhat sparse shrub up to 6 feet in height, mapleleaf viburnum readily develops suckers and forms thickets. Twigs are downy and brownish; the trunk is smooth and grayish, often with pale blotches.

LEAVES: Mapleleaf viburnum has several types of leaves; all grow oppositely on downy, ½- to ¾-inch petioles (stemlets). Some leaves are shaped like maple leaves, with three distinct lobes; others have indistinct lobes and are heart-shaped, while a few are oval in shape with no lobes at all. Most are 2½ to 4 inches in length and width, although some are smaller. All have deep veins; the top sides are deep green, while the undersides are paler and hairy, with tiny black dots. Most have coarse, sharp teeth all around except on the base, which may be rounded or notched; the tip is sharply pointed. In fall, the leaves turn reddish to purplish.

FRUIT: Egg-shaped drupes, ½ inch long, grow on thin stemlets in clusters on stalks that grow from the branch tips, beyond the last pair of leaves. Fruits are green, turning reddish before ripening to black. They are inedible.

SEASON: Clusters of yellowish-white flowers appear in early summer. The fruit is present much of the summer, ripening in late summer to early fall; it may persist over winter if not eaten by wildlife.

COMPARE: Because of its leaf shape, mapleleaf viburnum may be mistaken for a maple, particularly mountain maple (*Acer spicatum*), a shrub-like maple; however, maple fruits are dry, flat seeds with propeller-like wings. Guelder rose and highbush cranberry (pg. 150) also have maple-like leaves, but they are much leafier plants that are usually taller, and their ripe fruits are red.

NOTES: Thickets of mapleleaf viburnum provide food, as well as good nesting and escape cover for numerous species of birds and small mammals.

green = key identification feature

LARGE
WOODY SHRUB

OPPOSITE
LEAVES

LATE SUMMER
TO FALL

* see below

Hobblebush

Viburnum lantanoides

HABITAT: Rich, moist woods; along streams; in bottomlands and ravines; and on swamp edges. It prefers acid soil, and grows best in shady areas.

GROWTH: An open, straggling native shrub, up to 10 feet in height. Twigs are brownish to greenish, with scattered lenticels (breathing pores); as they mature, branches become gray and warty, eventually developing long, flat bark ridges. Longer branches arch downward, rooting where they touch the ground; this creates a tangled thicket that is known to trip unsuspecting hikers, giving rise to the common name, hobblebush.

LEAVES: Medium-green, coarsely textured leaves grow oppositely on thick, pale petioles (stemlets). Leaves are broadly oval, up to 8 inches long and nearly as wide; they typically have a heart-shaped base and a bluntly pointed tip. Edges have fine, closely spaced teeth; leaves are broadest at or below the midpoint. Main veins are deep, giving the leaf a wrinkled or pillowy appearance. Undersides are paler, with dense, star-like hairs (visible with a lens) on the veins. Leaves turn yellow, bronze or purplish in fall; often, leaves have multiple colors at the same time in fall.

FRUIT: Clusters of smooth, round drupes, each ⅓ to ½ inch across, grow on red stemlets rising directly from leaf axils; drupes have a small projection at the end and a single large seed. Ripe black fruits are edible raw or cooked, and are usually sweet. There are no toxic look-alikes in our area that are straggling shrubs with similar fruits and wide, pillowy leaves.

SEASON: White flowers are present from mid spring through early summer. The fruits are red most of the summer; a few in each cluster turn black by late summer, with the rest ripening to black in early to mid fall.

COMPARE: Wayfaringtree (*V. lantana*), found in our area only rarely in Indiana and Ohio, has clusters of red and black fruits, but there is a stalk between the cluster and the last pair of leaves; it is an upright plant with narrow leaves. Fruits are edible but bitter.

NOTES: Hobblebush provides a food source for birds and deer. It is listed as endangered in Kentucky. Some sources refer to this plant as *V. alnifolium*.

green = key identification feature

*specific KY locations not available

Wayfaringtree

LARGE
WOODY SHRUB

ALTERNATE
LEAVES

LATE SUMMER
TO FALL

Black
see below*

Purple
see below*

Chokeberries –OR– Aronia

Aronia spp.

HABITAT: Thickets, mixed-wood or hardwood forests, waste ground, urban parks. Tolerates a wide range of conditions, from dry to moist.

GROWTH: Three native chokeberry species grow in our area: black (*Aronia melanocarpa,* also listed as *Photinia melanocarpa*), purple (*A. prunifolia* or *P. floribunda*) and red (*A. arbutifolia* or *P. pyrifolia;* in our area, found in a few areas of western Kentucky). Chokeberries are leggy shrubs, up to 10 feet in height; black chokeberries are shorter. They are leafless near the base. Young stems are smooth and reddish-brown; branches have lenticels (breathing pores). Chokeberry suckers and often forms thickets.

LEAVES: Glossy, oval leaves with finely toothed edges are 2 to 3 inches long and two-thirds as wide. Leaves grow alternately on short petioles (stemlets). Midribs on top have small, hair-like glands (visible with a lens). Black chokeberry leaves are pale and smooth underneath; purple chokeberry leaves are moderately hairy below, and red chokeberry undersides are covered with fine white hairs. Leaves of all three turn reddish in fall.

FRUIT: A glossy, edible round pome with five distinct indentations in a star pattern on the base. Fruits are ¼ to ⅜ inch in diameter, and grow in small clusters on long, thin stemlets from the end of a branch. The fruit is acrid, but is tasty when sweetened; its seeds are so soft that they are unnoticeable. Black chokeberries are black when ripe; purple chokeberries, deep reddish-purple, and red chokeberries are scarlet red.

SEASON: Black and purple chokeberries are ripe in late summer to early fall; red chokeberries ripen in early to mid fall. Fruits of all three usually persist through winter.

COMPARE: Peking cotoneaster (*Cotoneaster acutifolius*) is a cultivated plant with similarly shaped leaves and black fruits that have a star-shaped indentation on the bottom, but its twigs and leaves are hairy; its fruits are reddish inside with four hard seeds. It is found in the wild in our area only occasionally in Indiana; its fruits are inedible.

NOTES: Aronia juice is popular in Europe as a health tonic.

green = key identification feature   *specific OH and KY locations not available

Black chokeberry

Red chokeberry

Purple chokeberry

Peking cotoneaster

LARGE
WOODY SHRUB

ALTERNATE
LEAVES

LATE SUMMER
TO FALL

Deerberry

Farkleberry

Deerberry –AND– Farkleberry

Vaccinium spp.

HABITAT: Deerberry (*Vaccinium stamineum*) and farkleberry or sparkleberry (*V. arboreum*) are native shrubs that are found in open, rocky areas with acidic soil, including hardwood or mixed-wood forests, streambanks, slopes and upland ridges. They prefer sun or dappled shade.

GROWTH: Farkleberry can grow to 30 feet in height, but is usually shorter; deerberry is usually shorter than 10 feet. Both are open shrubs that are twisted and gnarly, especially older specimens. Twigs are tan to greenish, and hairy when young; farkleberry stems may zigzag at leaf axils. Trunks of both have rough-textured brown or gray bark that is shreddy, patchy or fissured; the inner bark is reddish (visible between fissures).

LEAVES: Alternate, 1 to 2½ inches long with very short petioles (stemlets); leaves on the fruiting stems are usually smaller than others on the plant. Farkleberry leaves are leathery and glossy, with smooth or finely toothy edges; they are egg-shaped, broadest above the middle with a tapered base and a rounded tip that frequently has a small point at the end. Deerberry leaves are dull, with finely hairy edges; they are oval and tapered on both ends, with a pointed tip and whitish undersides.

FRUIT: Round, edible ⅜-inch berries grow singly or in clusters on thin stemlets from leaf axils. Ripe farkleberries are glossy black with a subtle crown on the base; they are usually dry, bitter and gritty. Deerberry have a more noticeable crown. They have a dusty bloom but vary in color; some ripen to purplish-black while others remain bluish or greenish even when ripe. Deerberry are also variable in eating quality; some are sweet with a spicy overtone and can be used like blueberries, while others are bitter or sour.

SEASON: Deerberry are ripe in late summer; farkleberry ripen in late summer to fall, and its leaves often remain green into the winter.

COMPARE: Unripe highbush blueberries (pg. 224) resemble deerberries, but ripe blueberries are intensely blue. Several inedible or toxic blackish fruits are found in our area, but none have a crown on the bottom.

NOTES: Eating quality varies tremendously; sample a few before harvesting.

green = key identification feature

Farkleberry

Deerberry leaves

Bluish deerberries

Greenish deerberries

LARGE SHRUB
OR SMALL TREE

ALTERNATE
LEAVES (TYP.)

SUMMER

Glossy Buckthorn

Frangula alnus

HABITAT: Open woods, wetlands, abandoned fields. Also found along roads, on the edges of power line cuts, next to ponds and streams, and along paths. Tends to form thickets. Also called *Rhamnus frangula*.

GROWTH: A large, multi-stemmed shrub up to 20 feet in height; sometimes appears to be a small tree. Branches often droop down over paths, making the colorful fruits very obvious. Twigs are reddish-brown with fine hairs. Bark of larger branches is smooth and grayish-brown, with noticeable lenticels (breathing pores) that are slightly raised.

LEAVES: Typically alternate, but may be opposite; smooth edges. Deep green above, lighter and slightly hairy below, with deep veins that form a V at the midrib, then curve near the edges to follow the contour of the leaf. Leaves are oblong with a short, pointed tip, 2 to 4 inches long and one-half as wide, widest at the midpoint or slightly toward the tip. Leaves turn yellow in fall, and usually remain on the plant longer than leaves of other shrubs or trees in the same area.

FRUIT: The ¼-inch berries grow in the leaf axils; often seen as a pair, but may also be single or in small groups. The berries are green with a small dot at the base when they first appear, developing a red blush and then changing to mottled red before ripening to black. The berries are mildly toxic and should not be eaten.

SEASON: Fruits are on the plant from early through late summer. Green, red and black fruits may all be present on the plant at the same time.

COMPARE: Common buckthorn (pg. 282) has opposite, toothy leaves that are more rounded. Dogwoods (pgs. 222, 232, 310) have leaves with similar veins, but the fruits are blue or white and are borne in umbrella-shaped clusters. Also see pg. 162 for information on other shrubs with multiple red fruits along the branches.

NOTES: This species was imported into the United States as an ornamental in the 1800s. It is considered invasive in many areas because it spreads rapidly, crowding out native plants.

green = key identification feature

Unripe fruits

**LARGE SHRUB
OR SMALL TREE**

**OPPOSITE
LEAVES**

**LATE SUMMER
TO EARLY FALL**

Blackhaw

Nannyberry

Blackhaw –AND– Nannyberry

Viburnum spp.

HABITAT: Blackhaw (*Viburnum prunifolium*) and nannyberry (*V. lentago*) are related, similar native plants that are found in openings and along edges of moist, well-drained hardwood and mixed-wood forests; they also grow along roadsides and streambanks.

GROWTH: Open and multi-stemmed, up to 20 feet in height. Stems are tan to reddish-brown; tips develop a long, pointed bud in fall.

LEAVES: The smooth leaves with finely toothed edges grow oppositely. Blackhaw leaves are oval to egg-shaped, 1 to 3½ inches long and two-thirds as wide; nannyberry leaves are more elongated and are up to 4 inches long but one-half to one-third as wide. Bases on both are rounded; tips of nannyberry leaves have long points, while those of blackhaw are more rounded. The petioles (stemlets) are a key point of differentiation between the two species; they are broad, with smooth edges on black-haw and wavy edges on nannyberry. Leaves of both turn maroon in fall.

FRUIT: Oval drupes, ⅜ to ½ inch long, grow on reddish stemlets in a loose cluster. The cluster grows directly from the tip of the branch; although individual stemlets may branch to give the appearance of a stalk, close inspection will reveal that there is no intervening stalk between the last pair of leaves and the base of the stemlets. Immature fruits are greenish-white, turning dull red before ripening to bluish-black with a dusty bloom. Ripe fruits are delicious raw or cooked; there are no toxic look-alikes.

SEASON: Blackhaws and nannyberries ripen in late summer to early fall; they often persist through winter and are edible even when shrivelled.

COMPARE: Withe-rod (pg. 226) has similar leaves and fruit clusters, but there is a stalk between the fruit cluster and the last pair of leaves. Rusty blackhaw (*V. rufidulum*) is very similar to blackhaw, with similar edible fruits, but its leaves are lustrous and have rusty-colored hairs underneath, particularly on the veins; in our area, it is found in southern Indiana and Ohio, and in much of Kentucky, particularly the Bluegrass Region.

NOTES: A delicious fruit, worth the trouble to remove the pit.

green = key identification feature

Smooth-edged petiole

Blackhaw

Nannyberry

Wavy-edged petiole, pointed bud

LARGE SHRUB
OR SMALL TREE

ALTERNATE
COMPOUND
LEAVES

FALL

Devil's Walking Stick

Aralia spinosa

HABITAT: This native plant is found in areas with moist, sandy or rocky soil, including disturbed areas, open woodlands, thickets, clearings, ravines, slopes and forest edges. It grows in full sun to partial shade.

GROWTH: A wickedly thorny large shrub or small tree, growing to 30 feet high. It has an open, flat crown; trees are top-heavy, often with few branches at the base. Twigs, stems and even the leaf stalks are armed with sharp thorns. Young stems are green; older bark is brownish to tan. Large clusters of white flowers are borne at the branch tips.

LEAVES: Twice- or thrice-compound leaves, up to 4 feet long and nearly as wide, grow alternately on leaf stalks that clasp the branch; from a distance, the leaves are open, with a lace-like appearance. Each branch of the leaf is 1 to 2 feet long, with five or six pairs of heart-shaped leaflets and a terminal leaflet that are 1 to 3 inches long and about half as wide. Leaves turn yellow or reddish in fall.

FRUIT: Oval drupes, ⅛ to ¼ inch long, grow in large clusters on lacy, reddish-pink or purplish stemlets at branch tips. The fruits are black when ripe, but are quickly eaten by birds, leaving behind the lacy network of stemlets. The fruits are inedible, and may be mildly toxic.

SEASON: Flowers appear in mid to late summer; fruits ripen in fall.

COMPARE: It is difficult to distinguish the native devil's walking stick from the related, but non-native, angelica (*A. elata*), found in our area only rarely in Ohio. Leaflets of devil's walking stick have a short but visible petiole (stemlet), while those of angelica attach directly to the stem. Also, the leaf veins of devil's walking stick stop short of the leaf edge, while on angelica, the veins extend to the edge. Another viciously thorny plant, Hercules' club (*Zanthoxylum clava-herculis*), is similar in overall appearance and thorniness; it is found south of our region. The clusters of small black berries with lacy pinkish stems on devil's walking stick resemble common elderberry (pg. 200), but the similarities end there.

NOTES: Tender young leaves can be cooked and eaten (Steve Brill).

green = key identification feature

Main stem

Thorns on leaf stalk

TREE

ALTERNATE
LEAVES

MID TO
LATE SUMMER

Black Cherry –OR– Rum Cherry

Prunus serotina

HABITAT: Sun-dappled hardwood and mixed-wood forests; edge habitat.

GROWTH: A tall, stately native tree, up to 90 feet high and 50 feet wide but typically smaller; when young, may appear as a small shrub. Young stems are reddish-brown or gray, with prominent lenticels (breathing pores); older bark is dark gray, with curling, scaly plates.

LEAVES: Smooth, glossy leaves are oval, with tapered bases and long, pointed tips; edges are finely toothed. Leaves are 2 to 5 inches long, one-half to one-third as wide, and dark green above, paler below. The base of the midrib on the underside has **fine reddish hairs** (visible with a lens); this is one of the easiest ways to positively identify a black cherry. Leaves grow alternately on long, pale petioles (stemlets).

FRUIT: Round, reddish-black drupes grow in **racemes** (long clusters of multiple fruits) from leaf axils. Fruits are about ⅓ inch in diameter; they are glossy but opaque. Fruit stemlets and the fruiting stalk are often reddish-purple. Black cherries are sweet and delicious, but the pit is fairly large in proportion to the flesh so the fruit is usually juiced, or pulped to make jam. There are no toxic look-alikes that are large trees, but there are several woody shrubs with inedible black fruits that could be confused with black cherries; please see below.

SEASON: Black cherries ripen in mid to late summer.

COMPARE: Chokecherries (pgs. 148) have edible fruits that grow in racemes, but leaves are proportionally wider and lack the hairs on the midrib. Buckthorn (pgs. 278, 282, 294) have mildly toxic black fruits; leaves of some are somewhat similar, but the fruits grow singly or in clusters from the leaf axils rather than in racemes.

NOTES: Black cherry leaves and pits contain hydrocyanic acid, a cyanide-producing compound. The leaves and pits should never be eaten, and care should be taken to avoid crushing cherry pits when juicing the fruits. Cooking or drying eliminates the harmful compound.

green = key identification feature

Hairs at base of midrib

TREE · ALTERNATE LEAVES · LATE SUMMER TO EARLY FALL

Hackberry

Sugarberry

Hackberry –AND– Sugarberry

Celtis spp.

HABITAT: These native trees are found in rich valleys and bottomlands, hardwood forests, waste ground, fencerows, ditches and urban areas. They prefer full sun and moist soils, but can adapt to drier areas.

GROWTH: Hackberry (*Celtis occidentalis*) is 40 to 60 feet in height with almost equal spread; sugarberry (*C. laevigata*) can be up to 80 feet. Lower branches of both often droop toward the ground. Young stems are reddish, with a zigzag habit; branches are brown, with light-colored lenticels (breathing pores). Bark on the trunk is dark gray; hackberry bark is ridged and warty, while sugarberry is warty with few or no ridges.

LEAVES: Rough-textured, dull green, alternate leaves are shaped like an elongated heart, with a sharply pointed tip; undersides are pale. Leaves are 2 to 5 inches long and one-half to one-third as wide; they are widest near the base, which is rounded and often slightly angled. Three of the leaf veins meet at the base of the leaf. Edges of hackberry leaves have large, pointed teeth except around the base, which has smooth edges; sugarberry leaves have smaller teeth, typically only on the top half.

FRUIT: Round drupes, ¼ to ⅓ inch in diameter, grow singly or in pairs on long stemlets from leaf axils. They are orangish-red in summer, ripening in fall. Ripe hackberries are purplish-black; ripe sugarberries are dull orangish-brown. The flesh is thin in comparison to the size of the pit; however, it is sweet and delicious. There are no toxic look-alikes that grow on trees.

SEASON: Fruits ripen in late summer to early fall, and they may persist through winter.

COMPARE: Dwarf hackberry (*C. tenuifolia*) is shorter and usually gnarly, with broader leaves that are somewhat rough-textured; in our area, it is found in much of central Kentucky, but in only a few counties of Indiana and Ohio. Black cherry (pg. 300) is a tree with small, round black fruits; however, its leaves are narrower, and the fruits grow in long clusters.

NOTES: Hackberries are often planted in urban parks and along streets because they are fast-growing shade trees and resist storm damage.

green = key identification feature

Ripe hackberries

Hackberry bark

Sugarberry bark

Sugarberries

TENDER
LEAFY PLANT

COMPOUND
LEAVES

MID TO
LATE SUMMER

White Baneberry
–OR– Doll's Eyes

Actaea pachypoda

HABITAT: This native plant grows in shady areas in moist hardwood and mixed-wood forests. Often found in dappled woods alongside bracken fern and large-leaved aster.

GROWTH: Two to four doubly compound leaves, each up to 15 inches long, grow alternately on the main stem; total height is 1 to 2½ feet. Flowers grow on a separate, leafless stalk that branches off one of the leaf stalks, and generally rise above the surrounding leaves.

LEAVES: Three large compound leaflets grow on each of the long leaf stalks attached to the main stem; each has three or five smooth, sharply toothed leaflets oppositely attached by short stalks.

FRUIT: Firm, glossy white berries about ⅜ inch long, slightly oval to round with a shallow vertical groove. Each berry has a **large, oval black dot at the bottom.** The berries grow in a cluster at the top of the thin flower stalk, and are attached to the stalk by **thick stemlets with slight knobs on both ends**; stemlets are **usually reddish-pink.** Baneberries are toxic and should never be eaten.

SEASON: Berries ripen in mid to late summer.

COMPARE: The related red baneberry (pg. 84) looks similar, but the flower stalk and berry stemlets are thin and greenish; those of white baneberry are much thicker and usually reddish-pink. Red baneberries generally have red berries, although they are sometimes white; regardless of color, the dot on the bottom of the red baneberry is much smaller than that on a white baneberry. Blue cohosh (pg. 212) has a similar form, but the leaves are rounded; fruits are larger and are blue when ripe.

NOTES: All parts of the plant are toxic. Ingestion of the berries leads to dizziness, vomiting or cardiac arrest; contact with leaves may cause skin irritation in sensitive individuals. Birds eat the berries with no ill effects, helping to disperse the seeds. Some sources list this as *A. alba*.

green = key identification feature

–OR–

WOODY VINE

SMALL WOODY SHRUB

ALTERNATE COMPOUND LEAVES

LATE SUMMER TO FALL

Eastern

Western *see below

Poison Ivy

Toxicodendron spp.

HABITAT: Moist areas with moderate sun, such as road ditches, open woodlands, fencelines, swampy areas and streambanks; also found in agricultural fields, sandy areas and disturbed sites.

GROWTH: Two varieties are native to our region: western (*Toxicodendron rydbergii*) and eastern (*T. radicans*). Western poison ivy grows as a shrub from 1 to 4 feet high, but can also appear as a tender leafy plant; eastern poison ivy is a climbing, perennial vine with stems that are often thick and hairy. Both have the classic three-part leaf configuration leading to the old saying, "Leaves of three, let it be."

LEAVES: Three-part leaves grow on the ends of long stalks attached alternately to the stem. Leaflets have irregular toothy or wavy edges; the petiole (stemlet) of the middle leaflet is longer than those of the side leaflets. Leaflets of western poison ivy are 2 to 4 inches long; those of eastern poison ivy are often up to 8 inches long. Leaves of western poison ivy turn red in fall; those of eastern turn yellowish.

FRUIT: The round, ridged berries, ⅛ to ³⁄₁₆ inch across, are greenish when immature, ripening to white or yellowish (see pg. 43 for a photo of eastern poison ivy in its green stage). Berries of western poison ivy grow in upright clusters near the main stem; those of eastern poison ivy grow from leaf axils in large, loose clusters. All parts of both plants are toxic and may cause a painful rash if touched; smoke from burning poison ivy can cause a severe allergic reaction.

SEASON: Berries develop in late summer, and persist through fall.

COMPARE: Atlantic poison oak (*T. pubescens*) is very similar to western poison ivy, but with hairy petioles and fruits; it grows in states to the east and south of our area. Black raspberry (pg. 262) and other *Rubus* have toothy 3-part leaflets, but they are brambles (vine-like shrubs) with thorny stems; fruits are compound drupes.

NOTES: The toxic compound in poison ivy, urushiol, remains active on everything it touches, until washed off.

green = key identification feature   *specific Indiana locations not available

Western poison ivy

Ripe berries of western poison ivy

PARASITIC
SUBSHRUB

OPPOSITE
LEAVES

EARLY
WINTER

Oak Mistletoe

Phoradendron leucarpum

HABITAT: This native plant, also called American mistletoe, is a parasitic sub-shrub that attaches itself to oak, Osage orange, red maple, hickory, elm and other hardwood trees; it has no intrinsic habitat of its own.

GROWTH: A small, evergreen shrub found growing on branches of hardwood trees, mistletoe is spread by birds, which deposit the seeds on tree branches either by wiping their beaks to remove the sticky pulp containing the seeds, or through droppings containing the undigested seeds. The seeds adhere to the branches and develop roots, which parasitize the host tree. Mistletoe has fleshy green stems, and grows in large, rounded clumps up to 3 feet across; it does not develop into a woody shrub-like plant, although older stems may develop a brown web-like covering that resembles bark. It is typically noticed as a cluster of green leaves high up in hardwood trees, after the host trees lose their leaves in fall.

LEAVES: Paddle-shaped, leathery leaves with parallel veins running from base to tip, are up to 2 inches long and about two-thirds as wide; they are widest above the midpoint. The tip is rounded, and the base is sharply tapered. Leaves grow oppositely on very short petioles (stemlets), and remain green all year.

FRUIT: Translucent, glossy white berries, ¼ to ⅜ inch across, grow in clusters on stemlets along the branches. The berries are juicy, with a single, ¼-inch-long seed and extremely sticky pulp. Berries and all other parts of the plant are toxic to humans.

SEASON: Mistletoe berries ripen in early winter, and remain on the plants through late winter, unless eaten by birds.

COMPARE: With its parasitic growth habit, its location high in trees, and its glossy white berries, mistletoe is unlike anything else found in our area.

NOTES: Mistletoe sprigs are used as holiday decorations; retailers sometimes replace the berries with plastic berries to prevent poisoning and to extend the shelf life of the decoration.

green = key identification feature

Oak mistletoe growing on
an Osage orange tree

LARGE
WOODY SHRUB

OPPOSITE
LEAVES

MIDSUMMER
TO EARLY FALL

Gray

Rough-leaved

Red-osier

Dogwoods with White Fruits

Cornus spp.

HABITAT: Three species of native dogwoods with white fruits inhabit our region: gray dogwood (*Cornus racemosa*), rough-leaved dogwood (*C. drummondii*) and red-osier dogwood (*C. sericea*). Gray dogwood is found in well-drained upland forests; the other dogwoods listed here prefer slightly damp soil, and are often found in swampy areas.

GROWTH: A bushy shrub, typically 4 to 6 feet in height but sometimes much larger; gray dogwood may grow to 15 feet. Often seen as a spreading thicket. The color of young stems helps identify the species: gray dogwood are bronze, rough-leaved dogwood are brownish-red, and red-osier dogwood are bright red or green splotched with red. Young stems are hairy.

LEAVES: Oppositely attached, 1 to 3 inches long and about one-half as wide, with smooth edges and silvery-green undersides with fine hairs. Distinct veins curve in towards the pointy tip. Leaf tops are smooth on gray dogwood, while those of rough dogwood leaves are coarsely textured; red-osier leaves appear puckered between the veins.

FRUIT: White, round drupes, ¼ inch across, with a small protrusion on the bottom; fruits of red-osier dogwood may be tinged with blue. The fruits are in a cluster at the end of a stalk that grows from a leaf axil or branch tip. The fruit stemlets of gray and rough-leaved dogwood are red, while those of red-osier are purplish. Dogwood fruits are inedible.

SEASON: Fruits mature from midsummer to early fall; gray dogwood ripens later than other dogwoods in the same area.

COMPARE: Roundleaf dogwood (pg. 222) has light blue fruits which may resemble those of red-osier dogwood; however, the leaves of roundleaf dogwood are wider and rough on the top, the stems are green with purple blotches, and the fruit stemlets are red.

NOTES: Dogwood fruits are eaten by many birds including cardinals, woodpeckers, wood ducks and upland birds; deer browse on the fruits, leaves and twigs. Dogwood is a host to the spring azure butterfly.

green = key identification feature

Gray dogwood

Red-osier dogwood

LARGE
WOODY SHRUB

OPPOSITE
LEAVES

LATE SUMMER
TO EARLY FALL

Common

Western
*see below

Common Snowberry –AND–
Western Snowberry

Symphoricarpos spp.

HABITAT: Two native snowberry shrubs are found in our area: common snowberry (*Symphoricarpos albus*) and western snowberry (*S. occidentalis*, also called wolfberry). Both are found in open woods, ravines and prairies, as well as on hillsides and along edges of grasslands. They prefer well-drained soil, but will tolerate somewhat damp conditions.

GROWTH: Bushy, rounded shrubs; western snowberry is typically 2 to 6 feet in height, while common snowberry is 3½ feet or less. Both often form thickets. Twigs are slender and reddish-brown, with fine hairs; older branches are gray and have shreddy bark.

LEAVES: Oval to egg-shaped leaves grow oppositely on short, hairy petioles (stemlets); edges are often wavy. Leaves of western snowberry are up to 4 inches long and roughly two-thirds as wide; common snowberry leaves are shorter, generally no more than 1½ inches long. Upper surfaces of both are blue-green to dark green, and may have scattered fine hairs; lower surfaces are generally hairy.

FRUIT: Roughly spherical, waxy white drupes, with a small floral remnant on the base, grow in tight clusters at the ends of branches or in leaf axils. Western snowberry fruits are round or slightly flattened, up to ¼ inch across; they are typically creamy white when young, turning purplish with age. Common snowberry fruits are frequently lumpy and misshapen, up to ⅜ inch across; they are usually brilliant white. Fruits of both are mildly bitter and are generally considered inedible; some sources list them as toxic.

SEASON: The fruits, which follow white to pinkish flowers, form in late summer, and may persist through winter on leafless branches.

COMPARE: Coralberry (pg. 140) is a related plant; its fruits are small and red.

NOTES: A winter food source for birds, including thrashers and many upland birds. Common snowberry is listed as endangered in Kentucky.

green = key identification feature   *specific IN locations not available

Common snowberry

Western snowberry

LARGE SHRUB
OR SMALL TREE

ALTERNATE
LEAVES

LATE SUMMER
TO FALL

American Snowbell

Styrax americanus

HABITAT: This native plant grows in swamps dominated by bald cypress or tupelo; also found in floodplain forests, oxbow lakes, moist open woods, wooded streambanks and areas that are seasonally wet. It requires moist soil and prefers partial shade.

GROWTH: A large woody shrub or small tree, up to 15 feet in height but often shorter. It has numerous thin branches, and an open, rounded crown. Bark is dark gray or brownish, and is smooth when young, developing shallow fissures with age; twigs are reddish-brown to grayish, and may be hairy. Numerous bell-shaped white flowers with five narrow, curled-back petals grow singly on short stemlets or in racemes (long clusters of multiple flowers) originating from the leaf axils; the fragrant flowers dangle beneath the branches, making a delightful display in late spring to early summer.

LEAVES: Smooth, dark green leaves grow alternately on short, broad petioles (stemlets); undersides are paler and typically downy. Leaves are up to 3 inches long and typically one-third as wide, broadest at the midpoint, with a tapering base and pointed tip. Edges often have shallow, irregular teeth above the base, but may be smooth. The leaves typically stand upright on the stems.

FRUIT: A round, leathery drupe, ¼ to ½ inch across and sometimes slightly flattened or lumpy. It has a green, five-lobed cap where it connects to the stemlet, and there is often a thread-like tail on the end. The fruit is greenish when immature, ripening to dull, opaque white. It is inedible.

SEASON: Flowers are present from late spring to early summer; the fruits ripen in late summer, and split open into three parts in the fall.

COMPARE: Bigleaf snowbell (*S. grandifolius*) is a southern plant with larger leaves; in our area it is found in a few counties in Indiana, where it is listed as endangered, and in a few counties in western and central Kentucky.

NOTES: Snowbell nectar attracts numerous butterflies, bees and other insects; its fruits are eaten by birds.

green = key identification feature

TREE

ALTERNATE
COMPOUND
LEAVES

SUMMER
THROUGH FALL

Poison Sumac

Toxicodendron vernix

HABITAT: Prefers shade and damp soil, and is often found at the edges of swamps or in poorly drained woods and bottomlands.

GROWTH: A small native tree up to 20 feet high, sometimes more like a large shrub, with red leaf stalks at the center of its compound leaves. Bark is grayish-brown and blotchy, with small raised bumps. Poison sumac often sends out branches from the base of the main trunk. Broken stems ooze a dark sap that is toxic.

LEAVES: Compound leaves grow alternately. Each leaf is 8 to 13 inches long, and has 7 to 13 leaflets on short petioles, growing on a red central leaf stalk. Leaflets are bright green, 2 to 4 inches long, smooth in texture with smooth, untoothed edges, and may be shiny on top. Poison sumac is very colorful in fall, with leaflets ranging in hue from yellow to orange to red to purple.

FRUIT: Round drupes are shiny and green when unripe, turning whitish-yellow by late summer; ¼ to ⅓ inch across. The fruits hang down in long, open clusters attached to leafless stems.

SEASON: Fruits ripen in late summer and may persist on the plant through winter, long after the leaves have fallen.

COMPARE: Smooth and staghorn sumac (pg. 182) have orangish to red fruits; leaves have more leaflets, and leaf edges are toothed.

NOTES: All parts of poison sumac are toxic, and can cause severe allergic reactions. The plant can be identified from a distance by the red compound leaf stalk, green to white fruits growing in a long cluster, and bright green or autumn-colored compound leaves. Stay away when you see these characteristics, as sensitive individuals may have a reaction merely by being close to the plant without even touching it. Burning the plants can cause respiratory distress in individuals a good distance away. Poison sumac is sometimes listed as *Rhus vernix*. No matter what it is called, this is a plant to avoid.

green = key identification feature

Fruit cluster

HELPFUL RESOURCES AND BIBLIOGRAPHY

Information on wild plants is readily available in books, magazines and on the Internet. Websites from University Extension Services, arboretums, colleges and institutions of higher learning are generally more reliable than personal websites. Here is a list of some websites and books which provide information that may be of interest to readers.

Websites

Early Detection & Distribution Mapping Systems, which shows current, known locations of invasive plants. (eddmaps.org)

Eat the Weeds, Deane Jordan. (eattheweeds.com)

Illinois Wildflowers Info, Dr. John Hilty. (illinoiswildflowers.info)

Kentucky Division of Forestry, Invasive Plant Threats. (http://forestry.ky.gov/foresthealth/Pages/InvasivePlantThreats.aspx)

Missouri Plants. (missouriplants.com)

The Nature Conservancy, Invasive Plants Distribution Maps for Ohio. (nature.org/wherewework/northamerica/states/ohio/science/art6279.html)

University of Connecticut Plant Database, Dr. Mark H. Brand. (hort.uconn.edu/Plants/)

Vanderbilt University, Department of Biological Sciences, Nashville, TN 37240. (cas.vanderbilt.edu/bioimages)

Virginia Tech, College of Natural Resources, Forestry Department, Blacksburg, VA 24061. (cnr.vt.edu/)

Books

Brill, Steven. *Identifying and Harvesting Edible and Medicinal Plants in Wild (and Not So Wild) Places*. New York: William Morrow, 1994.

Bryson, Charles T. and DeFelice, Michael S. *Weeds of the South*. Athens, GA: University of Georgia Press, 2009.

Elias, Thomas S. and Dykeman, Peter A. *Field Guide to North American Edible Wild Plants*. New York: Outdoor Life Books, 1982.

Horn, Dennis and Cathcart, Tavia. *Wildflowers of Tennessee, the Ohio Valley and the Southern Appalachians*. Auburn, WA: Lone Pine Publishing, 2005.

Marrone, Teresa. *Abundantly Wild: Collecting and Cooking Wild Edibles in the Upper Midwest*. Cambridge, MN: Adventure Publications, Inc., 2004.

Peterson, Lee Allen. *A Field Guide to Edible Wild Plants of Eastern and Central North America*. Boston: Houghton Mifflin Company, 1977.

Petrides, George A. *A Field Guide to Trees and Shrubs*. Boston: Houghton Mifflin, 1958.

Symonds, George W.D. *The Shrub Identification Book* and *The Tree Identification Book*. New York: Harper Collins, 1963 and 1958.

Tekiela, Stan. *Wildflowers of Ohio* (and *Michigan, Minnesota* and *Wisconsin*). Cambridge, MN: Adventure Publications, Inc., 1999–2001.

Thayer, Samuel. *The Forager's Harvest* and *Nature's Garden*. Birchwood, WI: Forager's Harvest, 2006 and 2010.

Wharton, Mary E. and Barbour, Roger W. *Trees & Shrubs of Kentucky*. Lexington, KY: The University Press of Kentucky, 1973.

REFERENCES CONSULTED BY THE AUTHOR

Websites

Flora of North America. (eFloras.org)

Trees, Shrubs and Woody Vines of North Carolina, Will Cook. (duke.edu/~cwcook/trees/)

U.S. Department of Agriculture, NRCS. 2008. The PLANTS Database. National Plant Data Center, Baton Rouge, LA 70874. (plants.usda.gov)

U.S. Forest Service, Washington, D.C. 20250. (www.fs.fed.us/)

Books

Dirr, Michael A. *Manual of Woody Landscape Plants*. Champaign, IL: Stipes Publishing, 1998 (fifth edition).

Kurz, Don. *Shrubs and Woody Vines of Missouri*. Jefferson City, MO: Missouri Department of Conservation, 2004 (second edition).

Nelson, Gil. *The Shrubs and Woody Vines of Florida*. Sarasota, FL. Pineapple Press, Inc., 1996.

Smith, Welby R. *Trees and Shrubs of Minnesota*. Minneapolis: University of Minnesota Press, 2008.

Sternberg, Guy and Wilson, James Wesley. *Native Trees for North American Landscapes: from the Atlantic to the Rockies*. Portland, OR: Timber Press, 2004.

Stevens, Russell L. and Coffey, Chuck R. *Trees, Shrubs and Woody Vines: A Pictorial Guide*. Ardmore, OK: The Samuel Roberts Noble Foundation, 2008.

GLOSSARY

Aggregate drupe: A fleshy fruit formed from a single flower, but composed of many drupes, each containing one seed; synonymous with compound drupe.

Alternate attachment: An arrangement of leaves in which individual leaves are attached to the stem in an alternating pattern, with some distance between each leaf. (*Compare:* Opposite attachment, Whorled attachment)

Annual: A plant which lives for one season only; reproduction is by seed rather than from roots. (*Compare:* Perennial)

Anther: The pollen-producing element of a flower.

Basal: Leaves growing at the base of a plant, often in a whorl or rosette.

Berry: A simple, fleshy fruit containing one or more carpels, each with one or more seeds; the seeds are relatively soft. (*Compare:* Capsule, Cone, Drupe, Pepo, Pome, Pseudocarp)

Blade: The entire grouping of leaflets, stemlets and central leaf stalk that make up a compound leaf. The word "blade" is also used to describe the wide, flat part of a simple leaf.

Bloom: A light-colored or waxy coating on a fruit or stem, that gives it a dusty appearance.

Bract: A petal-like structure at the base of a flower.

Bramble: A sprawling, vine-like shrub with arching branches that are generally thorny or prickly.

Cane: A flexible, woody stem; usually used to describe brambles such as raspberries.

Capsule: A dry, non-fleshy fruit that splits at maturity to scatter seeds. (*Compare:* Berry, Cone, Drupe, Pepo, Pome, Pseudocarp)

Carpel: Part of the ovary of a plant, containing ovules (eggs).

Cathartic: Purgative; causing diarrhea or vomiting.

Catkin: A spike-like structure with tiny unisexual flowers, often having a fuzzy appearance.

Clasping: A leaf that attaches directly to the stem, with no leaf stalk; the base of the leaf clasps, or slightly surrounds, the stem but does not extend beyond it. (*Compare:* Peltate, Perfoliate, Sessile)

Cleft: A linear depression with smooth edges.

Compound drupe: A fleshy fruit formed from a single flower, but composed of many drupes, each containing one seed.

Compound leaf: A leaf composed of a central leaf stalk with two or more leaflets. A compound leaf has a bud at its base; a leaflet does not. (*Compare:* Simple leaf)

Cone: A fruit consisting of scales arranged in an overlapping or spiral fashion around a central core; seeds develop between the scales. (*Compare:* Berry, Capsule, Drupe, Pepo, Pome, Pseudocarp)

Coniferous: A tree with needle-like or scale-like leaves (usually evergreen), whose seeds are contained in cones. (*Compare:* Hardwood)

Corymb: A flat-topped, umbrella-like cluster of multiple fruits, each growing on a stemlet that is attached to a single point on the central fruiting stalk; stemlets are varying in length so all fruits are on the same level. (*Compare:* Umbel)

Crown: A remnant of the flower, found on the base of some fruits; it looks like a circle of pointed, dried leaf tips. Also used to refer to the top of a tree or shrub, particularly one with a rounded appearance.

Cyme: A flat-topped cluster of flowers or fruits.

Dappled: A forested area that receives sunlight broken up by light leaf cover.

Deciduous: A tree or shrub whose leaves fall off at the end of the growing season. (*Compare:* Evergreen)

Dehiscent: A fruit that dries out and splits open to release its seeds; legumes are dehiscent. (*Compare:* Indehiscent)

Doubly compound leaf: A compound leaf consisting of two or more compound blades, attached to the central leaf stalk. Only the main leaf stalk has a bud at the base; the secondary compound leaves are not true leaves, and have no bud.

Doubly toothed leaf: Each leaf tooth has one or more smaller teeth, making for a jagged edge that alternates between coarse and fine teeth.

Downy: Having fine, soft hairs.

Drupe: A simple, fleshy fruit with a hard pit (stone); the pit typically contains one seed, but can contain more. (*Compare:* Berry, Capsule, Compound drupe, Cone, Pepo, Pome, Pseudocarp)

Elliptic: A leaf that is roughly oval in shape; ends may be pointed or rounded.

Endangered: A native plant whose populations have been depleted by animal predation or over-harvesting, or whose growing area has been reduced by pollution, habitat loss or over-competition from other plants.

Evergreen: Leaves that typically remain green; typically needle-like. (*Compare:* Deciduous)

Filament: A long stalk that holds the anther, the pollen-producing part of a plant.

Flower stalk: A separate stem that carries the flowers but no leaves. Synonymous with fruiting stalk.

Follicle: A dry fruit derived from a single carpel; follicles dry out and split open on one side only to release their seeds. (*Compare:* Legume, Nut)

Fruit: The ripened part of a plant that disperses seeds. (*See* Berry, Capsule, Cone, Drupe, Pepo, Pome, Pseudocarp)

Fruiting stalk: A separate stem that carries the fruits but no leaves. Synonymous with flowering stalk.

Gland: A cell, small organ or structure that secretes (discharges) minute amounts of fluids or other substances.

Hardwood: A broad-leaved tree whose seeds are contained in fruits or nuts. (*Compare:* Coniferous)

Indehiscent: A fruit that dries out but does not split open; nuts are indehiscent. (*Compare:* Dehiscent)

Introduced: A plant, often from Europe or Asia, that did not grow naturally in the wild in our area but was planted as an ornamental or a food crop; sometimes planted to control erosion or provide shade. Synonymous with non-native.

Invasive: A plant, generally non-native, that spreads rapidly and crowds out native plants, shades understory plants, or depletes soil of moisture.

Lance-shaped: A leaf that is long and slender, with sides that are almost parallel for much of the length.

Leaf axil: The point at which a leaf stalk (from a simple or compound leaf) joins the stem.

Leaflet: An individual leaf-like member of a compound leaf. A leaflet does not have a bud at its base; only true leaves such as the compound leaf and the simple leaf have a bud at the base.

Legume: A pod containing pea-like seeds; legumes dry out and split open to release their seeds. (*Compare:* Follicle, Nut)

Lenticel: A breathing pore, appearing as a bump or raised line in the bark of a tree or woody shrub.

Lobed leaf: A leaf that has several distinct sections, typically scalloped or pointed.

Midrib: The central rib of a leaf.

Mixed forest: A forest having both hardwood and coniferous trees.

Multiple fruit: A single fruit formed from multiple flowers that grow together in a cluster.

Node: A joining point between a leaf stem and the main stem or between two stems.

Non-native: A plant, often from Europe or Asia, that did not grow naturally in the wild in our area but was planted as an ornamental or a food crop; sometimes planted to control erosion or provide shade. Synonymous with introduced.

Nut: A large, dry fruit with a hard seedcoat, usually containing a single seed; nuts are indehiscent. (*Compare:* Follicle, Legume)

Opposite attachment: An arrangement of leaves in which individual leaves are attached to the stem directly across from one another. (*Compare:* Alternate attachment, Whorled attachment)

Ovary: A case containing carpels, which hold the ovules (eggs); a component of the pistil.

Paddle-shaped: A leaf that is narrow at the base, widening at or above the midpoint to a broad tip that is typically rounded.

Palmately compound: An arrangement of leaflets in a compound leaf, in which individual leaflets radiate from a central point, similar to fingers radiating from the palm of a hand. (*Compare:* Pinnately compound)

Pectin: A natural thickening agent found in apples and some other fruits; pectin helps jelly and jam "set" or thicken naturally.

Peltate: A leaf whose stem is attached on the underside, slightly away from the base of the leaf. (*Compare:* Clasping, Perfoliate, Sessile)

Pepo: A simple fruit with a tough rind developed from the receptacle. (*Compare:* Berry, Capsule, Cone, Drupe, Pome, Pseudocarp)

Perennial: A plant whose greenery, flowers and fruit die back each season, but which grows again the following year from the same root. (*Compare:* Annual)

Perfoliate: A leaf whose base extends slightly beyond the stem, giving the impression that the stem is growing up through the leaf. (*Compare:* Clasping, Peltate, Sessile)

Petiole: The stemlet that attaches a leaf, or a leaflet, to the stem or leaf stalk.

Photosynthesis: The process by which a plant converts sunlight to food.

Pinnately compound: An arrangement of leaflets in a compound leaf, in which individual leaflets are arranged either alternately or oppositely along the central leaf stalk. (*Compare:* Palmately compound)

Pistil: The female part of a flower, consisting of an ovary, style and stigma; usually in the center of the flower.

Pome: A simple fruit whose flesh is developed from the receptacle. (*Compare:* Berry, Capsule, Cone, Drupe, Pepo, Pseudocarp)

Pseudocarp: A simple fruit, such as a pome or pepo, whose flesh is developed from a part other than the ovary. (*Compare:* Berry, Capsule, Cone, Drupe, Pepo, Pome)

Raceme: A long cluster of multiple fruits, each growing on a stemlet that is attached to a central fruiting stalk; stemlets are equal in length. (*Compare:* Umbrella-like cluster)

Receptacle: An enlarged area at the base of a flower, just below the reproductive structures. In compound drupes, the receptacle is the core of the fruit.

Rhizome: An underground stem that produces lateral shoots and roots at intervals.

Runner: A shoot growing from the base of a shrub, capable of rooting along its length.

Sepal: A type of petal in the outermost group at the base of a flower; typically green and leaf-like.

Serrated: Finely toothed.

Sessile: A leaf that attaches directly to the stem, with no leaf stalk. (*Compare:* Clasping, Peltate, Perfoliate)

Simple leaf: A single, true leaf with a bud at the base of the leaf stem. (*Compare:* Compound leaf, Leaflet)

Sinus: The depression between lobes of a leaf.

Spadix: A club-like structure with many small flowers (later, fruits) clustered tightly together on a spike; usually partially enclosed by a spathe.

Spathe: A large petal-like structure, sometimes curled into a tube-like shape, that partially surrounds a flowering cluster called a spadix.

Stamen: The male part of a flower, consisting of the anther and filament; usually around the edges of the inside of a flower.

Stemlet: A secondary stem that connects a fruit or a leaf to the main stem.

Stigma: The part of a flower that collects and germinates pollen, which it then sends down the style into the ovules contained in the ovary.

Style: A long stalk that holds the stigma, which is the pollen-gathering part of a plant.

Subshrub: A perennial with a woody base and non-woody stems.

Sucker: A shoot that grows from the underground roots at the base of a plant; suckering plants often form thickets.

Tendril: A thread-like appendage, found on climbing vines, that coils around other plants or objects.

Terminal leaflet: The leaflet at the end of a compound leaf that has an uneven numbers of leaflets; other leaflets are paired.

Thicket: A dense cluster of shrubs, trees or brushy plants.

Toothed leaf: A leaf with multiple points (teeth) around the edge. Teeth can be sharply pointed or rounded. *See also* Doubly toothed leaf.

Trifoliate: A compound leaf with three leaflets.

True leaf: A simple leaf, or a compound leaf, with a bud at the base. (*Compare:* Leaflet)

Tuber: A thickened portion of an underground stem, containing buds from which new growth will sprout; the common potato is a well-known tuber.

Umbel: A rounded, umbrella-like cluster of multiple fruits, each growing on a stemlet that is attached to a single point on the central fruiting stalk; stemlets are equal in length. (*Compare:* Corymb)

Umbrella-like cluster: A cluster of multiple fruits, each growing on a stemlet that is attached to a single point on the central fruiting stalk. If stemlets are equal in length, the cluster is rounded (umbel); if stalks are varying in length, the cluster has a flat top (corymb). (*Compare:* Raceme)

Whorled attachment: An arrangement of leaves in which three or more leaves attach to a central point. (*Compare:* Alternate attachment, Opposite attachment)

INDEX

ABOUT THE AUTHOR

Teresa Marrone has been gathering and preparing wild edibles for more than 20 years. She was formerly Managing Editor of a series of outdoors-themed books, and is the author of *Abundantly Wild: Collecting and Cooking Wild Edibles in the Upper Midwest*, as well as numerous other outdoors-related cookbooks. Teresa also writes magazine articles on wild foods and cooking, and has taken up photography in recent years.

Wild Berries & Fruits Field Guide of Indiana, Kentucky and Ohio combines her various skills and interests into a clear, concise, easy-to-use book that helps the user appreciate the diversity of the various wild berries and fruits that grow in this region. Teresa lives in Minneapolis with husband Bruce and their Senegal parrot, Tuca.